ONLINE RESEARCH METHODS IN SPORT STUDIES

The internet and digital technologies have transformed sport and the way that we research sport, opening up new ways to analyse sport organisations, fan communities, networks, athletes, the media, and other key stakeholders in the field. This engaging and innovative book offers a complete introduction to online research methods in sport studies, guiding the reader through the entire research process, and bringing that process to life with sport-related cases and examples.

Covering both qualitative and quantitative methods, the book introduces key topics such as generating a research idea, implementing the research design, maintaining good ethical standards, and collecting, analysing and presenting data. It explains how to conduct online surveys, online interviews, and online ethnography in practice, and every chapter contains individual and group activities to encourage the reader to engage with real online research, as well as further reading suggestions to help them develop their knowledge.

Online Research Methods in Sport Studies is essential reading for undergraduate and postgraduate students, academics, and researchers with an interest in sport studies, and is a useful reference for practitioners working in sport or sport media who want to improve their professional research skills.

Jamie Cleland is based in the School of Management at the University of South Australia, Australia. His research often uses online methods to explore a range of social issues in sport.

Kevin Dixon is based in the School of Health and Life Sciences at Teesside University, UK. His research focuses on the social scientific study of sport and leisure cultures.

Daniel Kilvington is based in the School of Cultural Studies and Humanities at Leeds Beckett University, UK. His teaching and research focus on 'race', sport, and new media.

ONLINE RESEARCH METHODS IN SPORT STUDIES

Jamie Cleland, Kevin Dixon, and Daniel Kilvington

Routledge
Taylor & Francis Group

LONDON AND NEW YORK

First published 2020
by Routledge
2 Park Square, Milton Park, Abingdon, Oxon OX14 4RN

and by Routledge
52 Vanderbilt Avenue, New York, NY 10017

Routledge is an imprint of the Taylor & Francis Group, an informa business

© 2020 Jamie Cleland, Kevin Dixon and Daniel Kilvington

The right of Jamie Cleland, Kevin Dixon and Daniel Kilvington to be
identified as authors of this work has been asserted by them in accordance
with sections 77 and 78 of the Copyright, Designs and Patents Act 1988.

British Library Cataloguing-in-Publication Data
A catalogue record for this book is available from the British Library

Library of Congress Cataloging-in-Publication Data
A catalog record for this book has been requested

ISBN: 978-0-367-40813-8 (hbk)
ISBN: 978-0-367-40816-9 (pbk)
ISBN: 978-0-367-80930-0 (ebk)

Typeset in Bembo
by Apex CoVantage, LLC

CONTENTS

List of tables   *vi*

1   Introduction   1

2   Creating your online research question   8

3   Online research ethics   38

4   Online surveys   53

5   Online interviews   72

6   Investigating the online world   92

7   Analysing and presenting data   113

Glossary   *139*
Index   *145*

TABLES

2.1	Key Terms and Examples	17
2.2	Online Sources and Online Benefits	23
2.3	Qualitative and Quantitative Research	27
2.4	Benefits and Weaknesses of Online Research Methods	29
2.5	Probability Sampling Types	31
2.6	Non-Probability Sampling Types	32
6.1	Forms of Ethnography	96
7.1	Non-Parametric Tests	116
7.2	Parametric Tests	118

1

INTRODUCTION

Why research online?

According to the website datareportal.com, an online resource that specialises in providing the latest statistics for internet usage from across the globe, at the end of January 2019 there were close to 4.4 billion internet users out of a world population of 7.7 billion (see the list of references at the end of the chapter for the link to this report). Comparing this with January 2018, they report how an extra one million people per day accessed the internet over the course of just one year. They also illustrate how 5.1 billion people are mobile phone users (not all have internet access however), with nearly 3.5 billion of those who have internet access using a variety of social media sites (the average number of social media accounts per internet user was listed as nine). To illustrate why we believe the topic of this book is timely, we only have to compare the number of internet users in 2019 (4.4 billion) with the number in 2014 (2.485 billion) to see the significant growth of global internet consumption over just a five-year period. Indeed, the percentage share of internet time by mobile devices has also increased dramatically, from 26 percent in 2014 compared to 48 percent in 2019 (nearly doubling in that time). Adding to this, worldwide internet users are found to spend an *average* of six hours and 42 minutes online every day, with two hours and 21 minutes of this time spent consuming various social media sites (the top three most visited websites in the world are Google, YouTube, and Facebook).

Through examples of statistics like these, it is clear that the addition of tablets and smartphones to existing home, study, or work computers has vastly increased our immediate access to the internet in a short period of time. Of course, the internet is not universally available to all, but we do know that there are more digital communication gadgets in the world than there are people. As human beings we find the internet engaging for a multitude of reasons. Browsing the news or sport available online, shopping for holidays, clothes or other products, gaming, listening to music, watching videos or live events, as well as engaging in debate with other users on specific websites or social media platforms, are only some of the options that we have available.

By its very nature the internet is interactive with fluid boundaries in which researchers are increasingly looking to examine. As outlined by the Association of Internet Researchers (2012: 3), 'The internet is a social phenomenon, a tool, and also a (field) site for research'. From traditional methods of gathering survey questionnaires via post, in person or over the telephone, conducting interviews in person or over the telephone, and carrying out some form of visual observation of participants (either overtly or covertly), research can now be conducted from the comfort of your own home, library, university, or workplace quickly and at a relatively low cost. It also allows for larger sample sizes from a bigger geographical spread through the different ways in which the internet allows researchers to contact and interact with potential participants.

Online research can be both a tool for research and a venue for research that includes the use of information already on the internet, using it for recruiting participants, researching those engaging with various sites in some way and those who use it as a form of intervention (Harriman and Patel, 2014). By way of illustration from the statistics presented above, the everyday popularity of highly interactive social media sites as well as discussion forums, message boards, chat rooms and blogs to network, socialise, and debate through text, photographs, and videos have opened up many new ways for online researchers to access and collect user-generated data.

Not surprisingly, therefore, the internet has fundamentally changed our approach to communication and, in doing so, has provided significant amounts of data on a huge range of topics, including sport. This often takes place in a natural setting, such as across social media sites like Twitter, Facebook, and sports fan forums, but it can also include the collection and analysis of online newspaper articles and reports. Indeed, there is some form of online community that can practically suit any research interest. In this way, online research presents greater opportunities for those researchers new to methods being adopted in online settings as well as those who are more experienced in this field of research.

About this book

Given the long-established belief that research methods should be designed to incorporate modes of communication that are comfortable for the desired sample, it is fair to assume that the internet has a crucial place in the future of research. Many of the adverse myths surrounding the use of the internet for research projects are diminishing rapidly as online research is entering the mainstream. Researchers were once sceptical of researching online activities that were somehow degraded as inauthentic to physical 'real world' communications, but they now concede that the conceptual dichotomies that demarcate physical and online worlds are largely unhelpful (Gibbons and Dixon, 2010). New generations of researchers who have been schooled on digital technology are no longer fearful of its uses. They implicitly understand its strengths for the purposes of addressing a research aim(s) and objectives within a given project.

In a short period of time, the internet has revolutionised what we can research, what methods we can employ, and the communities we can reach, as well as widening the possibilities of who we can access and collaborate with. In short, the nature of research is changing, and this book sets out to critically examine online research methods in the context of what we simply term *sport studies*. Although we use this term across the book, we recognise within the content of our chapters the application to all of the relevant disciplines within the study of sport including sociology, culture, race, leisure, administration, governance, coaching, media, journalism, management, development, gender studies, business, health, tourism, physical activity and nutrition, exercise, psychology, and history.

The opportunities to conduct **primary** and **secondary** qualitative and quantitative research in the contemporary world of sport studies has been transformed, with new ways to analyse sport organisations, fan communities, networks, athletes, the media, and other stakeholders encouraging a range of innovative online methods to extract data. This book, therefore, attempts to offer an interdisciplinary approach that reflects on the opportunities presented by online research and how the internet has encouraged new and updated qualitative and quantitative methods of data collection and analysis. In doing so, at the heart of the book is the focus on three of the most commonly adopted methods of online research: online surveys (see Chapter 4), online interviews and focus groups (see Chapter 5), and online ethnography (see Chapter 6). These chapters will outline how the internet has become a cultural space full of opportunities to conduct research and explain the results within a theoretical and conceptual context.

As this book will outline, there are advantages and disadvantages to using the internet for online research. One of the more obvious advantages of using the internet to collect, analyse, and disseminate data (see Chapter 7) is the potential global reach and quickness of time it takes from what could be achieved through more traditional methods like face-to-face interviewing or paper survey questionnaires. However, there are also some disadvantages and ethical considerations (see Chapter 3) that need addressing before any data collection takes place, including privacy, confidentiality, informed consent, and the prevention of harm to participants as well as the researcher(s).

The writing of this very book has, not surprisingly, relied on online research. As you will see, the book examines contemporary examples of research in sport across each of the remaining six chapters, and the most up-to-date statistics at the time of writing where possible. Without websites, e-books, or online journals, this content would have proved very difficult to find, so we practice ourselves what we preach in this book. In addition, the book has also relied on online communication as its three authors are displaced by space and time. While Jamie Cleland lives in Australia, Kevin Dixon and Daniel Kilvington are based in England. So, could this book have been written without communicating online? Possibly, but it would have taken much longer to complete as the internet speeds up the process of communication. As authors, we regularly communicated via email when designing and producing this book and feel it will be a useful resource for undergraduate and postgraduate students in the broad discipline of sport studies as well as academic staff working in this field of research. We hope it also proves to be a useful guide for practitioners working in the sports industry, such as those involved in the media, sport for development and sports marketing.

Structure and content of the book

The structure of the book has been purposefully established to take the researcher on the journey from having no real research question in mind through the process of creating one and devising appropriate ethical considerations, to then identifying the best type of methodological approach needed to address the research aim(s) and objectives, before focusing on the analysis of data and the dissemination of the findings to the appropriate audience (whether that is undergraduate or postgraduate dissertation supervisors and examiners or through a funded report or other academic publication, such as a journal article, chapter, or book).

Chapter 2 focuses on the step-by-step process involved in creating an online research question. It discusses the research field and research topic whilst emphasising the importance of reviewing appropriate literature to aid the creation of research aim(s) and objectives. It then addresses the different methods available to online researchers and the types of questions that can be developed within a research study. The latter part of the chapter examines the process of sampling with regards to choosing participants for an online study and the various strategies available to researchers in addressing the research aim(s) and objectives of the project.

Chapter 3 concentrates on four main ethical considerations when researchers engage with the internet to collect, analyse, present, and store data. The first section outlines the ethical process by primarily concentrating on the role of ethics committees and codes of conduct now being implemented by relevant disciplines and organisations (internal and external). The second section addresses the importance of gaining informed consent irrespective of the difficulties sometimes involved when conducting online research. It highlights the importance of, where possible, informing participants about the research project, their role in the project, details of the research team and appropriate contact details, their right of withdrawal, and how their identity will be protected, so that the participant can make an informed choice as to whether to participate or not. The third section concentrates on harm and illustrates the importance of avoiding deception and protecting the participant as well as the researcher from any circumstance that could lead to some form of physical, psychological, or emotional stress or anxiety. The final section focuses on the public versus private debate about certain websites and the differences between them for the purposes of ethical data collection.

Chapter 4 focuses on the methodological approach of online surveys and presents five key sections to illustrate the opportunities and challenges researchers face. Firstly, it raises the importance of planning and the stages through which an online survey will develop before, secondly, addressing the area of sampling when identifying participants to take part. The third section concentrates on the questions within the online survey, in particular the importance of finding a balance between closed and open-ended questions to gain as much rich data as possible. The fourth section then illustrates some of the important strategic points when conducting the online survey, such as maximising the number of completions and the importance of undertaking some pilot research before wider distribution takes place. The final section addresses some of the potential problems that can be encountered by online surveys, namely under coverage and non-responses, and outlines ways in which this can be reduced whilst also discussing the importance of maintaining reliability and validity when undertaking an online survey to address the research aim(s) and objectives.

Chapter 5 explores the potential pitfalls and controversies associated with online interviews. It does this by concentrating on three main areas. First, it begins by explaining what interviews are and the various types available. Structured, semi-structured, and unstructured interviews will thus be defined and discussed in order to provide important contextual and background information on this research method. Second, the chapter then critically examines the multiple forms of online asynchronous and synchronous interviews available to researchers and offers some useful tips and guidance. The final section highlights a number of ways in which researchers can prepare for online interviews and puts forward some guidance on how online interviews can be carried out.

Chapter 6 focuses on online ethnography, otherwise known as netnography. This research method centralises observation as a research tool but often draws on other methodological approaches. Before exploring online ethnography, it is important to understand traditional ethnography as a research practice. Therefore, the opening sections of Chapter 6 focus on the emergence of ethnography as a research method, the ways in which it can be employed, and why it can be useful to researchers. It defines and discusses three standard approaches to ethnography: Non-participant observation, participant observation, and complete participant observation. This contextual discussion ends with an examination of the different ethnographic forms available, such as audience, auto-ethnographic, and institutional. Following this opening discussion, the chapter then covers how and why ethnography is used to investigate online spaces. Key aspects of online ethnography are highlighted, such as immersion and how to take, and analyse, research field notes effectively. The chapter also provides some guidance on how to enter online communities, online ethnography and research ethics, and how to conduct online ethnography reflexively. The latter part of the chapter discusses the advantages and disadvantages of online ethnography and offers a number of tips for those who wish to employ this research method in their own research.

Chapter 7 focuses on the analysis of data – a key area of any research project. It begins by exploring the various ways in which quantitative data can be collected. Hence, nominal, ordinal, ratio, and interval data are considered. Yet, the main focus of this chapter is on the analysis and presentation of qualitative data. It provides a step-by-step guide to how to analyse qualitative data, and how to generate, or develop, emerging codes (otherwise known as patterns or trends). Throughout this discussion, a clear and useful guidance for researchers who are analysing qualitative data is provided. The latter part of the chapter covers specific forms of data analysis approaches which researchers may use. These approaches include content analysis, discourse analysis, Interpretive Phenomenological Analysis, narrative analysis, thematic analysis, and grounded theory. This section also refers to various research projects within the field of sport studies whereby these approaches were adopted. By alluding to real-life projects, the reader can understand how this approach is used in action. The chapter ends by offering some important guidance on how to structure a research project as all of the sections come together for its completion and submission.

Developing your knowledge through key terms, activities, and questions

From qualitative to quantitative, from ethnography to netnography, from narrative to thematic analysis, research methods literature entails many terms that may confuse or puzzle debutant researchers. Learning about research methods, however, is not too dissimilar from learning about the rules of a sport. Take football, for example. None of us were born with a pre-existing understanding of the offside rule. However, once we read about it, see it in action, and discuss it with others, we develop an understanding. The offside rule is just one rule within the wider framework of rules governing football. The more time you spend in the game, the greater your understanding will be. Likewise, inexperienced researchers may be unfamiliar with the practices and processes involved in conducting online (as well as offline or more traditional) research projects. The only way to acquire the knowledge, and thus learn the research rules, such as appropriate sampling strategies, ensuring ethical standards of research, and how to analyse data effectively, is to familiarise yourself with them. Therefore, reading methodological literature and discussing your research ideas with your supervisor, colleagues, and peers will help you in gaining a comprehensive understanding of the rules, practices, and processes associated with online research methods. In order to help you fully understand the key elements involved with online research, we would like to draw your attention to the words emboldened across the chapters. We have identified these words as key terms and although we explain them in our chapters, we provide you a further definition in the glossary, which can be found at the back of the book. Whenever you have any doubt over any of the key terms feel free to browse through the glossary to aid your understanding.

Across each of the remaining six chapters of this book, we also provide a number of key resources and rhetorical questions to make you think clearly about the research journey all researchers go on: From identifying a topic, to gaining ethical approval, to devising questions and choosing your methodological approach, to collecting and analysing the data, to disseminating the findings in whatever format is required (such as through a specific piece of assessment, project, report, or other academic publication like a book, chapter, or journal article). We also offer advice in each chapter based on what we have read for the purposes of our own online research, what we have read for this book, and our own experiences of conducting online research. In doing this, we have created some individual and group activities throughout each chapter to help guide your own learning of some of the most widely used methods in sport studies research. We trust you will find the composition of chapters of value in your own research journey when using the internet for the collection of data.

References

Association of Internet Researchers (2012) 'Ethical decision-making and internet research'. Available at: https://aoir.org/reports/ethics2.pdf

Datareportal (2019) 'Digital 2019: Global digital overview'. Available at: https://datareportal. com/reports/digital-2019-global-digital-overview

Gibbons, T. and Dixon, K. (2010) 'Surfs up! A call to take English soccer fan interactions on the internet more seriously'. *Soccer & Society*, 11 (5): 599–613.

Harriman, S. and Patel, J. (2014) 'The ethics and editorial challenges of internet-based research'. *BMC Medicine*, 12 (1): 124.

2

CREATING YOUR ONLINE RESEARCH QUESTION

This chapter provides a step-by-step account of all the key considerations that relate to the design of a research question. It will begin by discussing several factors that should be considered when attempting to locate your research **field**. Following this, it looks at the necessary steps to take when narrowing your field into a feasible and manageable **topic**. It then emphasises the importance of relevant literature throughout and explores the various ways in which online and offline material can help focus a research question and develop knowledge of the topic area. The chapter will also discuss the different methodological approaches open to online researchers and provide guidance on which approaches suit which types of research questions. The penultimate section examines sampling and discusses the various strategies available to online researchers. Finally, the chapter concludes by using a marathon metaphor as we propose a suggested timeline for your research project.

KEY POINTS OF THE CHAPTER

- Understand how to generate, develop, and refine a research question.
- Identify the various types of online research available.
- Understand the difference between primary and secondary sources of information.
- Recognise the difference between theoretical and empirical research projects.
- Understand the purpose and necessity of consulting relevant literature.
- Awareness of the different qualitative and quantitative approaches in conducting online research.

- Identify the different sampling strategies available to online researchers.
- Reflect on the key considerations and milestones involved within online and offline research projects.

Finding your research field in the age of mass information

At the beginning of any research project, whether it is small or large-scale, the researcher must decide what to do and how to do it. This can often feel quite daunting, with researchers often asking themselves a number of key questions:

- How do I find my research field?
- How do I do something that is original?
- How do I focus my research question?
- Which methods are most suitable to my research question?
- Is the research going to be significant and meaningful?

These questions will occupy the researcher's thinking when positioned in the starting blocks at the beginning of their research project. At this point, they might feel apprehensive, nervous, and slightly overwhelmed. A regular cause for such anxieties revolves around **originality**, innovation, and the obsession to do something 'new'. There is mass information about the world, and this has reached unprecedented heights with the advent of the internet. For example, Dewey (2015) reports that there are an estimated 47 billion indexed searchable web pages, and if these were to be printed on physical paper, it would amount to approximately 305.5 billion pages. Add that figure to all published material not online and the information we have about the world is staggering, with new material being published every single day. Understandably then, the pressure to do something 'new' and original may feel like being presented with an impassable mountain. 'Newness' can often be misunderstood by researchers though. Of course, 'all research builds upon work done by others, and uses existing knowledge' (Gratton and Jones, 2010: 41), but it is highly unlikely that undergraduate students will develop completely original research on a topic that has never been investigated. Instead, new research usually always lends itself to older research.

At the outset of developing ideas, the following list illustrates some tips we feel are useful when trying to generate potential research questions:

- Try mind mapping or speed writing and see what ideas flow. Or, audio record yourself 'free-thinking' and listen back. Analyse what you have written or said and see if any themes or patterns emerge. This can help in focusing your topic and generating a research question.

- Use your supervisor or colleagues to help discuss your research ideas. Use their expertise, their knowledge, and guidance in narrowing down your research field. If you are aware of other academics, at other institutions, who have published on your topic, do not be afraid to contact them via email, LinkedIn, or Twitter.
- It is fundamental that you consult academic literature from the outset. What has been published in your field? What theories are most employed and relevant? Your supervisor or colleagues in the field will certainly be able to assist with highlighting recommended reading.
- Navigate the sports news for stories concerning your field. This is often overlooked by researchers. Moreover, you might want to access blogs, vlogs, or podcasts to understand what is current in your field.
- Finally, and arguably most importantly, your topic should be of interest to you. You are the one who is going to address it.

It is important to point out the difference between research **field** and research **topic**. The field might simply be sports advertising, social media, social class, or the Olympics. These areas might be of interest to you. But, at this stage, the nature and scope of your research is unclear and vague. The topic, on the other hand, is more focused as an angle has been identified. To summarise, while the field is broad and all-encompassing, the topic is narrow and focused. The following section will discuss key considerations when choosing your topic.

Choosing your topic

Once you have found your research field, broadly speaking, you then need to focus it. This focusing generally occurs as more literature is consulted. During the literature review phase, you should begin to generate some **research aims** in relation to what you want to achieve. Once you have identified some aims and **research objectives** (the steps you will take to answer your research question or a particular list of tasks you want to complete in order to accomplish the aim(s) of your research project), your research project should begin to take shape. You must be flexible and adaptive though as the literature review process may change certain aspects of your proposed project. What we present now are some of the key considerations a researcher must make before a topic has been decided upon.

Personal motivations

Researchers must be interested in their potential topic. Of course, the greater the interest, the more engaged and enthusiastic the researcher is likely to be. If the topic is one of great importance or intrigue, the research becomes more than just 'work', it can almost become a hobby to be enjoyed. For those of you who are undergraduate students, **dissertation** topics are often selected for personal reasons and this adds to the research experience more than those who have limited interest and passion for their topic.

Career aspirations also play a factor. For example, if a researcher desires to work in online sports marketing, choosing a question in this field affords them considerable time to critically investigate and understand this industry further. If qualitative work is to be undertaken, it may result in employment contacts and networks being created and developed. This deep and acquired knowledge can be showcased within CV's, cover letters, and job interviews, while networks could be utilised in locating future employment opportunities.

Your own knowledge and expertise must also be considered. When focusing your research topic, reflect on whether you already have some prior insight and understanding. What were your favourite college or university modules, units, or courses? What did you learn? What did you find particularly interesting and noteworthy? Your chosen topic might be very complex, can you do it justice in the allotted time you have before your set deadline?

Individual activity

- Mind-map, speed write or audio record your hobbies and/or topics you have enjoyed while studying. Do any patterns emerge?

Time

How much time can you devote to your project? This is crucial in determining the size and scale of what you wish to explore. You must consider the days you have available, and balance them alongside other commitments you may have. Gantt charts (you can download these online for free); physical or online diaries, planners, or calendars are excellent tools to foresee how many days, weeks, or months you can devote to your project.

Individual activity

- Decide on your time management platform, e.g. online Gantt chart, online calendar, etc.
- Cross out all the unavailable dates, e.g. birthdays, extra-curricular pursuits, lectures, and seminars, part-time work, etc.

- Set yourself long-term (complete research project), mid-point (complete methodology draft), and short-term (access relevant e-books) targets.
- Start to populate the diary, calendar or chart with 'research project time'. It is advisable to have some form of routine so 'research project time' becomes a habit. That said, remember, 'life happens' and you should always afford some level of flexibility in your working pattern.
- Try to give yourself daily or weekly tasks to complete and tick them off as you go. Doing this will further ensure that you meet the set deadline.

Geography

The internet transcends place, space, and time, meaning that researchers are now able to investigate communities, organisations, and nations outside their locale. For example, researchers can explore the global nature of cricket fandom by analysing relevant content on social media platforms. Online surveys can be circulated globally to understand why participants play certain sports. From behind the keyboard, we can now undertake a **content analysis** of sports coverage by the media around the world, either historically or in the present day.

Economics

Researchers using offline qualitative methods would regularly have to allocate money for travel and sometimes accommodation expenses. Online researchers, on the other hand, arguably have fewer financial constraints to consider. As an online researcher, you must have access to the internet, which can, of course, cost money. While most online research tools are free, such as online survey websites (Survey-Monkey and Google Surveys) and audio recording software (in-built within android and smart phones), transcription and data analysis software can be expensive.

Access

Is it possible for you to gain access to the participants or group you intend to reach? Can you obtain the information required? When setting your aims and objectives, access must be considered. For example, a lack of access often encourages the researcher to adopt a different methodological approach.

Significance

Whatever you decide to research, there must be some level of significance involved. Why is your research worthwhile? Why is it important? During an investigation, many researchers encounter the 'so what' moment. If you are struggling to see the point or the main goal of your research, then some further thought and planning is required. Put simply, there must be a strong justification for your work. It must matter and be significant in some way. Does it attempt to offer something different, new, or address a gap in the research field? Your research might attempt to put forward policy recommendations for reform or solutions to a problem. Research that attempts to initiate positive change is often labelled **impact research**.

Individual activity

- Carry out some online research into the work and activism of Celia Brackenridge. Her research into women in sport, and the physical and sexual abuse suffered by young people by sports coaches, generated significant impact. Can you list the ways in which her research generated impact?

Clarity

You should be able to articulate your research topic in one sentence. If you struggle to simplify your investigation into a single sentence, you are perhaps trying to do too much; the work may be too broad, too ambitious, or unclear. As we illustrated earlier, it is good practice to propose some overall research aims or questions, followed by several objectives. By including this clearly in your study's introduction, the reader is immediately aware of what the work intends to achieve.

Group activity

This activity allows you to have a go at formulating clear and significant research questions. Here are some words and phrases that you might want to include:

- *To what extent. . .*
- *A critical investigation of. . .*
- *In what ways have. . .*
- *An analysis of. . .*
- *Researching. . .*
- *Investigating. . .*
- *Exploring. . .*
- *Examining. . .*

- *How. . .*
- *Why. . .*

> **Field:** Gambling
> **Topic:** Online sports betting and spectatorship.
> **Working title (potential question):** To what extent is online, in-play sports betting affecting how fans engage in contemporary live sports consumption?
> **Clear and significant:** The key words are online sports betting, affecting, and fans. Therefore, it is a clear and focused question. The study attempts to assess how online sports betting affects or influences how fans watch or engage with sport. The significance depends on how well the question is researched and answered. Nevertheless, it is arguably a worthwhile topic as potential themes might include addiction, mental health issues, and the technological ease of contemporary gambling facilitated by betting websites. This study could promote recommendations for reform to help potential gambling addicts, based on the evidence presented. This would certainly help justify the project and emphasise its significance as impactful research.
>
> In small groups, see if you can generate working titles that are clear and significant from the below **topics**:
>
> - Sports injury, elite athletes, and recovery.
> - Boxing, masculinity, and exclusion.
> - Activism, sport, and social media.
> - Cycling and gender.
> - Fitness apps and gamification.
>
> Compare your **working title** with other groups and discuss in what ways they could become clear and significant research projects.
>
> When you have read Chapters 4, 5, and 6 in this book, return to this activity to check whether your research question still works, and consider what online research methods you would employ to help answer the proposed question you have devised.

Originality

The obsession with originality can often be a headache for any researcher. You are not expected to choose something that has never been explored before as that would be rather difficult. Instead, what angle or approach can you take that offers some level of difference or 'newness' in making a contribution to knowledge in the field?

Research in sport

'Tackling social media abuse: Critically assessing football's response to online racism', by Kilvington and Price (2017).

What was the aim of the research?

This aim of the study was to critically comprehend the level of online racism within football and uncover what football's key stakeholders: The Football Association (FA), Kick It Out, The Professional Footballers' Association (PFA), and professional football clubs were doing to challenge this issue.

What were the methods used?

The study employed a multi-method approach to gather empirical data. Telephone and face-to-face interviews were carried out with key officials at the respective bodies. Moreover, an open and closed-ended online survey was sent to all 92 professional football clubs. Kilvington and Price wanted to understand whether football authorities considered online racism towards players, fellow fans, and clubs a problematic area of the game; what mechanisms were in place to help victims of online abuse; what, if anything, they are individually and collectively doing to challenge it; and what should be done in the future to help further tackle this issue. Four officials were interviewed at Kick It Out, one from the PFA, one from a professional club, but the work failed to gain an interview with anyone from the FA. The work only received a total of seven online survey responses. The article theoretically drew on past studies and included quantitative data to help illustrate the growing problem of online abuse within a football context.

What were the key findings?

Using a constructivist grounded theory framework, the following four themes were generated: (1) football's key stakeholders suffer from a lack of communication. Each organisation is attempting to challenge this issue, however, due to the lack of contact between each body, work is being replicated. Establishing relationships or a 'football and social media working group' would help pool resources, thus strengthening the challenge; (2) Kick It Out are arguably doing the most work to tackle this issue, yet, they remain extremely under resourced in terms of staff and finance. More time and investment must be put into this issue if it is going to be comprehensively addressed; (3) key stakeholders are struggling to gain access to clubs and players. Players are often the victims and help and support must be available. Conversely, they are sometimes the aggressors and must be educated on social media usage. The research also found that club safeguarding officers themselves struggled to gain access to first-team players; (4) players who had suffered racial abuse online appeared less inclined to raise the issue in fear of playing the 'race card'. A streamlined and clear support system should, therefore, be in place for players suffering from online racial abuse.

Why is this research original?

There is plenty of research involving online trolling (Alkiviadou, 2019; Bliuc et al., 2018), online hate speech within sport (Farrington et al., 2015; Kilvington and Price, 2019), and backstage discourses of racism within sport (Feagin and Picca, 2007; Hylton and Lawrence, 2016). That being said, here is why the project by Kilvington and Price is original:

- It theoretically advances the field. It applies literature from psychology regarding the factors that exacerbate and reduce online abuse, and it draws on sociological literature concerning different spaces for racist discourse. It therefore attempts to push the theoretical understanding of online abuse further than has been done before.
- It offers a specific, case study approach. There is very little research on football and online racism, and therefore it addresses a gap in the field.
- It includes a multi-method approach by using qualitative and quantitative data.
- It puts forward solutions to help further challenge this problem in football. It has the potential to generate impact through the conclusions that were identified.

Individual activity

- This research in sport example by Kilvington and Price (2017) presented above is original but small-scale. It does not mean that future researchers are banished from researching online racism within football. Far from it. Instead, work that builds on existing literature is encouraged and there are various ways in which the field of online racism within football, and sports generally, can be developed. Can you think of ways in which this study, and the wider field of online racism in sport can be developed further?

When your topic is chosen

Bang! The gun has fired. The marathon is officially underway! You have selected your field thanks to the ongoing consultation of literature; a process that has helped you in selecting your topic. You might not have your research question perfected, but you may have identified several research aims and objectives and even formed a **working title**. This necessary preparation means that you have a solid base and foundation for your research (just like a marathon runner who has trained effectively). At this stage, it is important to consider what type of research you want to undertake. But first, see Table 2.1 below, as it provides a reminder and overview of some of the key terms that we have covered so far in this chapter, as well as some helpful examples.

TABLE 2.1 Key Terms and Examples

Key Terms	Overview and Example
Research Field	A field, or area, in which to study, e.g. cycling, online trolling, disability. This is very broad and lacks an angle or focus. This is the first step though in the process to reaching your research question. *Example: Social media.*
Research Topic	The focus has now been generated and the angle of the research is established. This usually takes place while the literature is being consulted. *Example: Social media and football fandom.*
Research Aim(s)	This refers to your overall research goals. The emphasis here is on what you want to accomplish, not how you will accomplish it. Some projects include one research aim while others list several aims. *Example: To understand the ways that fans develop a connection and relationship with their football clubs through social media platforms.*
Research Objectives	Your objectives are the stepping stones used in helping you find out your research aims. Broadly speaking, research objectives refer to what researchers intend to achieve in the project. The list of objectives should be highly focused and closely related to your aim(s). *Example: (1) To assess the different online approaches employed by clubs in communicating with their fan base; (2) To find out which of the approaches results in greater online fan engagement; (3) To create recommendations for football clubs regarding the most effective ways to engage fans online.*
Working Title	This is a rough question. It is flexible. During and after the literature review stage, working titles often adapt or change. *Example: A critical investigation of how English Premier League clubs use social media to interact with fans.*
Research Question	The final question. This is sometimes settled upon or finessed at the end of the project. Depending on the researcher's pre-study knowledge of the field or topic, this might be established much earlier in the research process. *Example: A critical investigation of how social media is used by English Premier League clubs to create and strengthen relationships among their fan base.*

Types of research

Research can be classified in many ways. There are several major types of research you can undertake. Choosing which type depends on your aim(s) and objectives, how the data will be collected, and how such data will be analysed.

Historical

Historical research is best defined as 'the systematic and objective location, evaluation, and synthesis of evidence in order to establish facts and draw conclusions about past events' (Walliman, 2011: 9). It allows researchers the ability to reflect on past events and comprehend these findings in the context of the present. For instance, solutions from past events could be applied to contemporary settings. Moreover, it could help explain or predict emerging or future trends. And, historical research allows for a revaluation of prior data, theories, and generalisations about the past.

Exploratory

Exploratory research takes place when there is 'little or no prior knowledge of a phenomenon' (Gratton and Jones, 2010: 6). This research attempts to explore the phenomenon as you seek early clues. It also aims to gain some familiarity with some relevant concepts and recognises patterns or trends from the data without prior explanation. Exploratory research can be followed up with further research that examines the generated hypothesis (if there is one).

Comparative

Comparative research compares 'people's experiences of different societies, either between times in the past or in parallel situations in the present' (Walliman, 2011: 11). Abeza et al. (2017) used a comparative approach when critically exploring how social media operates as a relationship marketing tool amongst American professional sports teams. They used **netnography** to understand how professional teams, across different sports, used social media to communicate with their fan base (this methodological approach is discussed in more detail in Chapter 6).

Descriptive

Descriptive research 'describes a particular phenomenon, focusing upon the issue of what is happening, or how much of it has happened, rather than why it is happening' (Gratton and Jones, 2010: 7). Bennet and Jonsson (2017) used a descriptive approach to highlight the numbers of discriminatory social media messages posted across an English professional football season. While they note that approximately 134,400 instances of discriminatory abuse occurred on social media platforms over an eight-month period, just within an English professional football context, they do not use any qualitative empirical methods to understand why this might be happening.

Explanatory

This research type, simply put, refers to *why* something happens. As noted above, Bennet and Jonsson (2017) quantified the extent of the problem of social media related football abuse. Their work stated what was happening, not why. Kilvington and Price (2017, 2019), on the other hand, drew on Bennet and Jonsson's (2017) quantitative data but attempted to explain why this phenomenon was happening by focusing on primary and secondary sources. This work could be developed even further by conducting interviews with the perpetrators of online abuse to critically understand their motives, although researchers must acknowledge the problems and ethical dilemmas with this approach.

Predictive

Predictive research 'forecasts future phenomena, based on the interpretations suggested by explanatory research' (Gratton and Jones, 2010: 7). Based on the evidence and data collected, researchers attempt to envisage what will happen in the future. If the prediction relates to something detrimental or negative, solutions can be put forward to try and prevent predicted problems.

Impact

Impact is the buzzword of contemporary academia. Traditionally, researchers were trained to generate or test new ideas, not put them into practice. However, impact research is now a major (and growing) element of academic practice. Reed (2016: 9) notes that impact refers to 'the beneficial changes that will happen in the real world . . . as a result of your research'. There are five main avenues for impact:

1   Instrumental impact (e.g. actual changes to policy);
2   Conceptual impact (e.g. new understandings);
3   Capacity-building impact (e.g. training of students or professionals);
4   Attitudinal impact (e.g. increased willingness to engage in new collaborations);
5   Enduring connectivity impact (e.g. follow-on interactions such as joint proposals, shared workshops, lasting relationships).

As Reed (2016: 4) suggests, impact might be achieved by 'changing policy or practice, licensing [a] patent, or changing public perceptions'. Importantly, the researcher must attempt to evidence the impact. This can be achieved, for example, by using oral testimonies or interviews, surveys, or correlative data, which illustrate that a change has occurred.

Individual activity

- Find the online staff profiles of your lecturers, colleagues, or research collaborators. Have they generated any research impact? If so, how?

Feminist

Feminist research relates to any piece of research that involves theory and analysis that illustrates the differences between the experiences of men and women. There is no singular or general feminist methodology, but the methodology is critically informed by theories of gender relations.

Critical race theory

Critical Race Theory (CRT) emerged in United States (USA) law schools as activist scholars such as Derrick Bell, Kimberle Crenshaw, Richard Delgardo, and Patricia Williams began to highlight and challenge the contemporary manifestations of 'race' and racism in society. Although CRT originated from legal studies in the USA, its appeal spread and it is now on the radar of other disciplines including economics, anthropology, and sociology. For Hylton (2009: 22), CRT is a framework used to 'examine the racism in society that privileges whiteness as it disadvantages others because of their "blackness"'. CRT therefore aims 'to challenge inequalities and strive towards social justice' (Kilvington, 2016: 7). Despite being labelled 'a theory', it is arguably more of a methodological approach. Yes, 'race' is used as a critical lens to theoretically underpin the work, but its tenets such as storytelling, transdisciplinarity, and social justice and transformation are centred at every stage of the research process. Embracing a CRT position, then, means that the researcher acknowledges the societal world is not meritocratic, and that racialised inequalities and privileges exist. Methodologically, the researcher is not neutral and unbiased, as they enter the research with an anti-racist and activist stance. This affects how the research is conducted.

In summary, through this brief overview of the different types of research, choosing the type for your own research largely depends on your research aim(s) and objectives.

Group activity

In groups, decide which research type or types are best suited to the following research questions:

1   To what extent is online sports gaming a male dominated space?

2   A critical examination of Paralympics coverage in broadsheet and tabloid newspapers from 1960 to 2020.

3   A critical investigation of sexism within boxing fan online forums.

4   To what extent is football fans expressions of Islamophobia across social media platforms a growing concern for football's key authorities?

5   In what ways do the English, Spanish, French, and German men's national football teams attempt to build belonging and community with fans on Twitter, Facebook, and Instagram?

Primary and secondary research

A distinction can be made between **primary** and **secondary** research projects. **Primary research** refers to data that has been gathered for a particular project. So, if you intend to conduct primary research, you might conduct a survey, an interview, or a content analysis to generate original data. **Secondary research** refers to research where no original data has been collected; instead, the research relies on already published sources. Secondary research is often called a 'literature based' study. Most, if not all, studies include secondary research, notably in the literature review chapter or chapters, as it enables the researcher to understand and showcase what studies have been published previously, what theories are applicable, and what gaps exist in the field.

Theoretical and empirical research

In addition, and relatedly, you can choose between **theoretical** or **empirical** research. **Theoretical research** relies on critically investigating findings from existing literature (secondary) and using it to develop or shape new theories and explanations. For example, you might want to use Pierre Bourdieu's work on social, cultural, symbolic, and economic capital to help explain the historical under-representation of African-American head coaches in the National Football League (NFL). On the other hand, **empirical research** generates and tests out new ideas through the collection of data (primary). An empirical approach, then, may apply Bourdieu's work as a theoretical framework (secondary) but would undertake online interviews (primary) with key figures in the NFL, such as current and former players and coaches, to help critically understand this phenomenon. We agree with Gratton and Jones (2010: 8) in that 'if at all possible – support your findings empirically through the collection of primary data', rather than relying on secondary sources.

The literature review

You are firmly underway in the marathon. The literature review stage, which should commence as early as possible, is a fundamental part of the process. Walliman (2011: 137) emphasises the importance of consulting relevant literature:

Reviewing the literature is essential, not only in providing context for the research subject and specifically limiting and identifying the research problem, but also in providing you with important information for subsequent parts of the research investigation, such as alternative theoretical standpoints and suitable research methods.

Literature reviews are integral to almost all research investigations. As Moore (2006: 111) notes, 'Just about all projects require a review of published literature and internet resources to position the work in its proper context'. Literature reviews conclude when you have reached a level of **saturation**, meaning that no new ideas or theories are being raised in response to your research aim(s) and objectives.

EXAMPLE

- A literature review is the study's foundations. Like a sports stadium, its foundations must be solid in order to build on. While the literature review is the base of the study, the methods become the stands while the results and discussion become the roof. If any of these three areas are incomplete, or incorrectly built, then the project will crumble. Without a solid base, it would be impossible to build on.

The purpose of a literature review

It is important to consider the purposes of a literature review as we use the existing literature in different ways and for different reasons. This section should help you understand what literature to search for, how to use it, and why it might be useful. Literature reviews help the researchers in the following ways:

- *Provide familiarity.* You can familiarise yourself with the subject. Read around the topic and attempt to acquire as much knowledge as you can.
- *Develop your awareness of relevant theories and concepts.* If you are exploring power relations in sport (consider Foucault); audience consumption and taste (consider Bourdieu); football hooliganism and fan practices (consider Giulianotti). If you complete your project without referencing or showing an awareness of key literature or theories in your field, your work is likely to be flawed. You must consider the extent to which such works can help theoretically underpin your research.
- *Focus your question.* Of course, without consulting the literature, you cannot generate a research question as you would be unaware of previous research and what the findings were. Building up your knowledge on your topic allows you to generate clear and significant research objectives to address the research question.

- *Understand the extent of past research.* Once you know the past, you can form the foundations to build new work.
- *Identify past methods.* What methods have been employed and what settings have been investigated in previous research? Has a particular group, space, or environment been overlooked? Paying close attention to past methodologies allows you to propose new and innovative ways to gather data.
- *Comparison.* Can you assess the successes of prior research designs? Can you evaluate the findings of past research? Consider how your work might compare to relevant prior studies.

Different sources of online information

As this book is focused on the internet, this section will explore various online sources of information as well as the benefits of using online platforms to find relevant material. It starts by presenting Table 2.2 to outline appropriate online sources and the benefits of these to researchers.

TABLE 2.2 Online Sources and Online Benefits

Online Sources	Online Benefits
E-Books	Most academic books published in recent times will be released as e-books and can often be located via Google Scholar as well as your university library. The simplest benefit of e-books is that it saves you a trip to the library! Despite some preferring physical books due to their touch and feel, e-books can be viewed on a bigger screen, font sizes can be enlarged, and users can cut and paste, or screenshot, relevant sections and save them in electronic files. Moreover, some e-books offer a Text-To-Speech (TTS) function, allowing you to listen to the work. This can be particularly useful for students with dyslexia, visual impairment, and other reading difficulties. Finally, environmentally, they are welcomed as they are paperless.
Online Journals (sometimes known as e-journals)	Most journal articles will be electronically accessed by students as most universities do not let students take out journals from their libraries. Online journals should be consulted within your research as they offer the most up-to-date research within your field. Some journals delay physical publication for up to two years following electronic release so it is advisable to consult online journals during your project. Using your university library site, you will be able to gain access to online journals and find relevant works by using the search tab. For precise searches, you can enter the title of the paper or the author name, while for imprecise searches, likely to take place at the beginning of your research, you can enter key words or relevant authors and scroll through the hits. You can read the abstracts before deciding how relevant the article might be for the purposes of your own research.

(Continued)

TABLE 2.2 (Continued)

Online Sources	Online Benefits
Online Newspapers (sometimes known as e-newspapers)	Online newspapers are excellent sources to find out the latest discussion, news, and 'facts' within your field. Reports might even give you some ideas regarding your research focus. Conversely, via your library site, it is likely that you will also be able to access newspaper articles, which have now been electronically uploaded, from decades ago. This can be particularly useful when thinking of undertaking a *historical* or *comparative* research project. The Conversation is an excellent website and is highly recommended (the articles are written by academics in a very accessible style).
Online statistics (sometimes known as e-statistics)	Using your university library, you should be able to access online statistics websites. For instance, the Leeds Beckett University library portal allows access to the Office for National Statistics (ONS), Gov. uk, Eurostat, Statista, among other platforms. We recommend using and citing statistics from official sources, e-books, or online journals as opposed to from journalists or non-academic websites.
Social media and online forums (e.g. online newspaper or fan website)	Scrolling through social media and online forum comments can give you some indication of public opinion regarding past, present, or future events. Reading posts can sometimes help generate research topics and clarify your focus. Sometimes, these comments alone can be the basis of investigation. Moreover, if you follow a widely published academic, blogger, or journalist who has written on your topic, why not send them a message asking for their help and guidance.
Search Engines	We cannot escape search engines. We live in the age of Google. There are approximately 3.5 billion Google searches every single day. Google searches are inescapable within the research process. If you are investigating how the sport media frame Formula One racing driver Lewis Hamilton, you would most certainly use Google to find relevant articles or Google image to collate images (online newspapers could also be accessed using your library website). At the very beginning of your research project, Google will regularly be used to help locate background information or find potential interviewees and relevant groups. Google Scholar, an academic search engine, is a useful tool too.
Blogs and Vlogs	What are bloggers and vloggers currently saying about your research topic? Read and watch their posts and see whether they raise anything valuable in relation to your studies. They might offer some historical information or recent developments which you could investigate further using more official and trustworthy sources.
Online streaming, e.g. YouTube, Box of Broadcasts	You might be able to access some audio-visual material through your library service. Box of Broadcasts is an excellent service that allows you to stream content which has been recorded for academic purposes, i.e. television, film, radio programmes. Conversely, search YouTube to see what documentaries, interviews, programmes, or other relevant content has been uploaded. Relevant Ted Talks are particularly useful to view when in the early planning stages of your research project.

(Continued)

TABLE 2.2 (Continued)

Online Sources	Online Benefits
Wikipedia	A word of warning: Refrain from referencing Wikipedia in any of your work. Meyer (2013) notes that approximately 90 percent of its top editors are male, and largely white, meaning that entries are framed through a certain (white, male) lens. Nonetheless, when attempting to get a handle on something extremely complex, such as a theory you intend to apply to your work, there is little harm in scanning through Wikipedia to try and understand the basics of the theory. Once you have some understanding of the theory or concept, the next step would be to access relevant e-books or online journals.
Email	Use your email to make or maintain contact with your supervisor, research collaborators, and/or academic librarian as he or she will be able to highlight any relevant literature. Of course, email can facilitate this, but meet them person too if possible.

As Table 2.2 illustrates, it is clear how the internet has changed how researchers collect background information and conduct literature reviews. The internet is worldwide and contains masses of data, but this vast amount of information can result in false leads, time wasting, and inaccurate data. To mitigate some of these potential pitfalls, it is important to test the validity of online sources.

Testing the validity of websites

Now that you have accumulated more knowledge and have a greater understanding regarding the wide array of online sources available to researchers, we can return to an earlier group activity and build on our prior discussions.

Group activity continued

Revisit the below questions once again. Select ONE of them. Choose THREE of the above online sources and locate ONE relevant source for each of them, e.g. one e-book, one online newspaper article, one YouTube video.

1   To what extent is online sports gaming a male dominated space?
2   A critical examination of Paralympics coverage in broadsheet and tabloid newspapers from 1960 to 2020.
3   A critical investigation of sexism within boxing fan online forums.

4   To what extent is football fans expressions of Islamophobia across social media platforms a growing concern for football's key authorities?

5   In what ways do the English, Spanish, French, and German men's national football teams attempt to build belonging and community with fans on Twitter, Facebook, and Instagram?

Discussion

- Is your source theoretical or empirical?
- What are the main aim(s) of your source?
- Which of your sources is the most useful and why?

E-books and online journals have been peer reviewed and are thus trustworthy sources of information. Content from wider internet sources, in contrast, must be held to a higher degree of critical scrutiny. We recommend using the checklist below when scrutinising online sources of information.

- Check the website and where the data sources are from. Compare this data with other sources for proof. Websites ending in 'ac' (academic) or 'edu' (education) refer to content from universities or colleges and therefore have some academic credibility. If it is 'com' or 'net' then the information might be questionable and untrustworthy.
- Who is the author of the work? Are they an expert or part of a reputable organisation? How detailed and comprehensive is this information? If works are cited, such as in a bibliography or as web links, check them out.
- Is the information objective? Or is it one-sided? Pressure groups, marketing organisations, and some bloggers tend to write persuasively as they attempt to convey a certain argument. Always consider and investigate the counter arguments.
- When was the work published? Internet sources usually include an upload date. If you are searching for recent statistics, for example, aim to find material as up-to-date as possible.

Choosing your methods

Methods allow you to tell a story. But what that story is, and how it is told, depends on the methods you choose. Research methods are the tools of the trade.

EXAMPLE 1

A carpenter building a snooker table cannot achieve this without the relevant tools such as a saw, a hammer, sandpaper, varnish, etc. The methods represent the tools. But, it is essential that the carpenter knows how to use these tools properly and effectively. The greater the understanding and experience of using these tools, the better the end product.

Advice: Read methodology literature in advance of designing your study.

EXAMPLE 2

If a recreational jogger decides to 'get fit', they must develop a strategy. Their tools might be appropriate running footwear, a treadmill, or a fitness app. These tools should help in achieving their end goal of raising their fitness levels. Yet, the end success depends on the runner's determination and dedication.

Advice: Commit to your research. Dedicate sufficient time for data collection.

EXAMPLE 3

Finally, if a researcher intends to explore how feelings of belonging and community are developed through sport, they must select the most appropriate methods. Qualitative, rather than quantitative, methods might be more suitable for this topic as they allow the researcher to delve deeper and gain 'richer' data, understanding the *why*. Appropriate methods might include open-ended questions in online surveys, online focus groups, or online interviews.

Advice: Although no perfect methodology exists, certain methods lend themselves to certain research questions. Always be aware of this.

Researchers have a general choice between qualitative and quantitative methods. **Ethnographic** research can also be undertaken which can combine both types (see Chapter 6). As outlined in Table 2.3 below, quantitative and qualitative research can be characterised in different ways.

TABLE 2.3 Qualitative and Quantitative Research

Quantitative Research	Qualitative Research
Relies on numerical data to measure social phenomena to produce trustworthy 'facts'	Social reality is a lived, subjective experience that is always in process
Attempts to answer the 'what' is happening	Attempts to answer the 'why' and 'how' something is happening
Employs statistical analysis to comprehend casual factors	Tends to use smaller samples, or 'cases'

(Continued)

TABLE 2.3 (Continued)

Quantitative Research	Qualitative Research
Centres objectivity as the researcher is 'detached' from the participants under investigation	The research environment is often 'natural'
Able to replicate	'Richness' of data
Generalisable	Affords flexibility in the data collection
Adheres more to a positivist framework	Adheres more to an interpretivist framework

Single or multi-method approaches

Researchers must consider whether their research question can be best answered using a single methodological approach or multiple methods. Although using a single method can be perfectly justified, especially for small-scale research projects, most researchers undertaking longer-term projects would argue that a multi-method approach is most appropriate. Using multiple methods allows the researcher to gain a more comprehensive understanding of the phenomena in question. Multi-method researchers are able to build up a fuller picture that offers breadth and depth. Yet, you must be able to justify why you have selected more than one method. Ask yourself: What extra benefit does an additional methodological approach give? How will this deepen your data and findings? How will the methods complement one another?

Research using the internet

When the empirical data collection phase begins; you are firmly underway with your research project. In many cases, this commences around the halfway point. This is a pinnacle moment in any study as the data you 'uncover' is only as useful as the observations you have made, the questions you have asked, or the survey you have designed. To select the most appropriate research method, or methods, certain factors must be considered:

- Refer to your research aim(s) and objectives. Is a quantitative, qualitative, or multi-method approach most suitable? Do you want to understand individuals' experiences of a phenomenon (qualitative) or how often a phenomenon is occurring (quantitative)?
- Consult the academic literature on research methodologies. Read widely and broadly at the beginning but once your method is selected, read deeper into your chosen method.
- Always be aware of the limitations of your method and contemplate how any weaknesses can be mitigated.
- Consult primary sources in relation to your topic. Focus on their methods and reflect on how your approach offers originality.

TABLE 2.4 Benefits and Weaknesses of Online Research Methods

Benefits of Online Research Methods	Weaknesses of Online Research Methods
Convenient and saves time	Truthfulness of responses (if participants are anonymous and invisible)
Cost effective	The setting in which the participant participates in is often unknown. The participant, therefore, may be distracted or multi-tasking while participating in the research.
Investigate hard to reach populations	Ethical issues as some online methods can be obtrusive
Possibility of gaining larger sample	Reliant on technology working
Possibility of gaining more diverse sample	Need sufficient IT skills
Online interviews have instant transcription	Research requests via social media or email can be easily ignored
Online survey data can be instantly coded	Participants may exit before the end leaving the data incomplete

- As noted previously, consider the time, money, and geographical constraints.
- Consider your attributes or personal qualities. Would you feel comfortable or confident interviewing a participant one-on-one or leading a focus group? Some researchers prefer non-human interaction opting for content analysis or online surveys instead.

Depending on your research focus then, you could employ surveys, interviews, focus groups, content analysis, and visual analysis to answer your question. All of these approaches can be conducted online, e.g. email survey, Skype interview, online focus group, content analysis of Twitter hashtags, and a visual analysis of Snapchat stories. Researchers can therefore use online methods to collect and gather data. In some cases, an online approach might be more suitable, convenient, or quicker than a traditional method such as face-to-face interviews or a postal survey. As Gaiser and Schreiner (2009: 5) state, 'online researching has opened new environments to researchers that move beyond traditional research and challenge some of our notions of what it means to research'. Yet, we must remain critical and be aware of the advantages and disadvantages of online research methods when designing our projects, as shown in Table 2.4.

Researching online worlds

It must be emphasised that there is a difference between research that uses the internet to collect data, and research that investigates the internet and its communities. The internet provides a platform whereby meaningful social interactions take place. According to Gaiser and Schreiner (2009: 5), 'any place where people interact online represents a potential place where interactants can be observed and discussions can be analysed'.

Online observations can be conducted to critically examine how communities interact, perform, and mobilise. Longer-term online observation is defined as online **ethnography** or netnography. Netnography is best suited for larger scale research projects. As Chapter 6 will outline, online observation is most successful when employed within a multi-method approach.

Research in sport

'Online belongings: Female fan experiences in online soccer forums', by Hynes and Cook (2013).

What was the aim of the research?

The research investigated the experiences of women who engage in and contribute to soccer online forums. Because soccer is traditionally considered to be a male pastime, Hynes and Cook sought to examine notions of inclusion and exclusion, masculinity and femininity, and perceptions of authentic and inauthentic fandom. In addition, Hynes and Cook also explored the differences between online and offline personas.

What were the methods used?

In addressing the research aim, the multi-methodological approach consisted of online interviews and observations. A total of 16 online interviews were carried out. The participants were members of online forums that were created by clubs and fan groups to help facilitate discussion and an analysis of soccer and other, unrelated topics. Online observation of the forums was used to generate lines of inquiry which were further explored within the online interviews.

What were the key findings?

Hynes and Cook note that soccer remains ideologically masculine. The game is played and watched by 'real men' as the nostalgia of the 'glorious past' is consistently referenced. They continue, noting that female fans are positioned in an ongoing 'struggle for respect, acceptance, and ownership of the masculinised game' both in physical and online spaces (2013: 108). Because women are perceived to contradict the 'true fan' image, female fans within online forums modify expressions of their gender identity to feel comfortable and gain acceptance within the masculinised, heteronormative online space.

Sampling

A **sample** refers to the selected number of cases within a **population**. The population refers to all the cases that could be included. A population can consist of objects, people or events, e.g. rugby clubs, rugby fans, the Rugby World Cup. It might be possible to conduct online interviews with everyone involved with a local rugby club (total population). Yet, it would be impossible to conduct online interviews with all rugby fans or everyone involved at a Rugby World Cup. Therefore, a sampling strategy must be created 'whenever you can gather information from only a fraction of the population or a group or a phenomenon which you want to study' (Walliman, 2011: 185).

There are basically two types of sampling – **probability** (random) and **non-probability** (non-random). Probability sampling is used when the sample size is too large. It is also employed more for quantitative based studies. There are four main types of probability sampling, as outlined in Table 2.5.

TABLE 2.5 Probability Sampling Types

Sampling Type	Description
Random Sampling	Random sampling arguably offers the most reliable and representative results as every member of the population has the same chance of being selected. The easiest way to do this is simply drawing names or numbers out of a hat. The 'hat' can be digital as 'random number' apps exist, for example, and can be used to generate names and numbers until the desired sample size has been reached.
Stratified Random Sampling	This method is used to divide the population into relevant subgroups, e.g. age, sex, ethnicity, religion. You could divide your population into 'gym user' and 'non-gym user'. Then, you would randomly select a 50 percent gym user and a 50 percent non-gym user sample from your population. This enables your initial sample to be contemplative of the subgroups that are within the population.
Cluster Sampling	This refers to groups being randomly selected rather than individuals. If you wanted to explore tennis clubs and the importance of economic capital, you could randomly select several tennis clubs and question all the members at the clubs. Several clusters should be selected to help achieve some level of generalisability.
Systematic Sampling	This method chooses every *K*th case to produce a sample size from the population. For example, if you are examining fan reactions to an athlete's social media post, it might contain thousands of comments. Systematic sampling may opt to select every fifth or tenth post.

Non-probability sampling is said to rely on the judgements of the researcher. Unlike probability sampling, this qualitative and interpretive approach is rarely used to make generalisations of the total population. Yet, theories and models can still be developed and shaped from non-random samples, as shown in Table 2.6.

TABLE 2.6 Non-Probability Sampling Types

Sampling Type	Description
Convenience	The sample is selected because it is convenient. The researcher may select a certain location or group of people due to ease of access. This is often observed within undergraduate dissertations as students choose to interview their fellow course mates. Despite convenience sampling being tempting, it should be avoided unless it can be fully justified. It can, however, have some benefits when ethnographic or online ethnographic approaches are considered.
Critical	The researcher chooses a sample perceived as 'critical' when attempting to understand the phenomenon in question. This is often used when the sample size is either small or hard to access. This approach lends itself to generalisable research results.
Emergent	The researcher selects participants as opportunities begin to emerge. This method can be useful when little is known about the field or topic in advance of the study.
Nominated	Participants or informed experts recommend future participants. The researcher can choose to contact or ignore the nominated participant.
Opportunistic	The researcher selects samples as they emerge, capitalising on any unexpected opportunities. The researcher may not expect to find a lead or an interviewee at that time, but the opportunity is seized. This relies on being in the right place at the right time.
Snowball	The researcher identifies several key participants at the beginning of the study. The researcher then asks said participants to identify relevant participants who may be able to assist with the research. Like a snowball rolling down a hill, your sample therefore gets bigger and bigger. **Gatekeepers** are often used within a snowball sampling framework. These influential figures are effectively your 'research sponsors' – they vouch for you and grant you access to new participants. Because you have an 'insider' assisting you, new participants might be more likely to co-operate and assist with your research.
Theoretical	Following every new step, such as a new online interview or a newly completed online survey, the researcher examines this new data which informs their next move. Theoretical sampling therefore follows the emerging **codes** (see Chapter 7).
Total population	The researcher studies an entire population of people who share a common experience or characteristic. Investigating the total population can only be achieved when the population is relatively small, e.g. a local sports team of relevance, witnesses, or a particular event or incident.

(*Continued*)

TABLE 2.6 (Continued)

Sampling Type	Description
Typical	The researcher selects the sample based on the belief that they are 'typical' of a particular theory. This approach allows the generalisation of other typical, normal, or average cases.

Your marathon: A suggested timeline

This chapter has covered all the essential aspects when it comes to creating and developing your research question. Although there is no set or standard way of conducting research, we would suggest the following timeline for empirical research projects for both undergraduate and postgraduate students, as well as academics and researchers:

THE START LINE

Consider which field you would like to investigate and begin to conduct some background research. Browse online material and peruse key pieces of literature and texts.

THE GUN FIRES

The race is underway when you have confirmed your field and generated a research topic, or angle, because of the initial background research. A clear research aim, or aims, should be created to help ensure the topic remains focused. You begin to consider your research objectives, which should be closely related to your research aim(s). A flexible working title may be created. The literature review continues.

STEADY PROGRESS

The literature review is in full swing and you are beginning to critically understand the gaps in the field, what cases or populations might have been overlooked, what methodological approaches might be suitable, and what theories might be relevant. Your research aim(s) and objectives are now firmly in place. This phase only concludes once you reach saturation. Your flexible working title may very well be modified. Begin drafting your literature review.

APPROACHING THE MIDWAY POINT

Around a third to half way through the marathon you should have completed a first-draft of your literature review which allows you to demonstrate critical knowledge of the field, an awareness of prior research, and which relevant theories and concepts, if any, apply to your work. At this stage, it is essential that methodology reading commences and initial ideas are developed regarding how to best answer your question. Books (such as this one) should prove very useful for you. You should see a direct correlation between your literature review reading and your methodological ideas as the literature should inform the avenues you follow in your methods. More time should be devoted to your methodological phase if you intend to conduct empirical, rather than theoretical, research.

FIRMLY IN YOUR STRIDE

As you reach the midway point you should have a clearly developed methodological strategy and firm understanding of your sample. As you pass the midway point it is important to begin collecting data (this phase can commence sooner depending on the scope and scale of the project).

ENTERING THE FINAL THIRD

At this point, you have acquired a critical understanding of your field, cultivated a clear and significant research question or working title, designed a justifiable methodological approach, and conducted research seeking to accomplish your research aim(s) and objectives. From a qualitative framework, it is best practice to code the data as it is generated so emerging codes can be investigated as an ongoing process (see Chapter 7). While you are analysing the data, and generating potential themes and key findings, you should begin to draft your methodology chapter. This chapter is usually written in the past tense and it is advisable to offer some critical reflexivity when discussing your methodological process and practice.

THE FINAL PUSH

Moving into the final third, it is important that you have analysed the data and generated some key themes and ideas. This is often considered the 'fun bit' or the easiest part of the research project as you are presenting your own primary research (if you have undertaken an empirical research project). Remember, your literature review chapter or chapters should not be a long-forgotten memory, instead, they are central to your results and discussion chapters (see Chapter 7). Ask yourself: Does your work advance knowledge in the field? Does it support or contradict prior work? Can the theories and concepts you examined earlier be applied to your empirical data? Your results and discussion should therefore explicitly link and connect with the discussions and arguments made in your literature review. The results and discussion chapter is the last significant chapter you will need to write and it is important to devote sufficient time to this. If this were a marathon, a first draft of this chapter should be completed approximately around mile number 20 of the 26 miles, at the latest.

THE FINISHING LINE

With the finishing line in sight, you have successfully completed at least one draft of your substantial chapters, e.g. literature review, methodology, results and discussion. Your supervisor or research collaborators will provide constructive feedback and subsequent drafts can be completed when possible. It is advised to write the conclusion next, and the introduction at the very end. These chapters are not as detailed or comprehensive as your main chapters but you still need to devote adequate time to them. Ensure that your introduction includes a rationale for the research topic and some clear research aim(s) and objectives so the reader is clear of your goals and set outcomes from the beginning. Your conclusion should be concise and highlight your key findings that address the original aim(s) and objectives, possible solutions, research limitations, and future research ideas.

CELEBRATION

Research projects are a marathon, not a sprint. Remember to pace yourself. Time management is crucial. But at the end of the project, as you pass the finishing line, you should be proud of yourself and celebrate your victory. If you follow this suggested timeline, and read the subsequent chapters of this book, therefore becoming fully informed about the various online methodological approaches available to researchers, we are confident that you will succeed and pass that all important finishing line – and that calls for a celebration!

Conclusion

This chapter has offered a step-by-step approach regarding the key factors related to choosing research questions. It has adopted a running metaphor to help explain that research projects are not a sprint, but in fact a marathon. Research projects take considerable planning and do not begin when the first word is written; they actually commence when you first begin to think about your field and topic. We have emphasised several considerations such as time, access, and geography when formulating your research topic. Researchers must also take into account the type of research that they wish to undertake, and this very much depends on the aim(s) and objectives of the research.

Although there is no such thing as a perfect or fool-proof methodology, there are certain methodological approaches that suit certain types of research questions. It is always worth bearing this in mind when beginning to plan your methodological approach. Moreover, while some projects might be better suited to a single method, others lend themselves to multi-method approaches. Regarding the latter, you must be able to justify why you have selected a second or third method and how the additional methods allow you to understand the research phenomenon more comprehensively.

This chapter has also discussed theoretical and empirical work, as well as primary and secondary research. As we have expressed earlier in the chapter, we do advocate for work that offers something new, substantial, and original, which is usually generated by undertaking empirical research. Secondary research is unavoidable though and must be included in your work as it informs your literature review, methodology, as well as the results and discussion. Yet, as we note, some caution must be afforded when using online sources. As researchers, our job is to maintain a critical mindset, and to critically scrutinise the information we consume. So, ask yourself whether the sources you use are trustworthy and if not, why not.

The activities you have undertaken in this chapter have hopefully allowed you to create or further develop, or refine, your own research question. These practical exercises have offered you the chance to consider, and critically reflect on, a variety of key considerations regarding research projects such as research types, approaches, and sampling strategies. This is an important chapter in your research journey and as you continue through the subsequent chapters of this book, you may well find yourself returning to this chapter as you develop further critical knowledge regarding online methodological approaches to collecting online data.

References

Abeza, G., O'Reilly, N., Seguin, B. and Nzindukiyimana, O. (2017) 'Social media as a relationship marketing tool in professional sport: A netnographical exploration'. *International Journal of Sport Communication*, 10 (3): 325–358.

Alkiviadou, N. (2019) 'Hate speech on social media networks: Towards a regulatory framework?' *Information & Communications Technology Law*, 28 (1): 19–35.

Bennet, H. and Jonsson, A. (2017) 'Klick it out: Tackling online discrimination in football'. In Kilvington, D. and Price, J. (Eds.) *Sport and Discrimination*. London: Routledge, pp. 203–214.

Bliuc, A.M., Faulkner, N., Jakubowicz, A. and McGarty, C. (2018) 'Online networks of racial hate: A systematic review of 10 years of research on cyber-racism'. *Computers in Human Behavior*, 87: 75–86.

Dewey, C. (2015) 'If you could print out the whole internet – How many pages would it be?' *The Washington Post*, 18 May. Available at: www.washingtonpost.com/news/the-intersect/wp/2015/05/18/if-you-could-print-out-the-whole-internet-how-many-pages-would-it-be/?noredirect=on&utm_term=.7d5310a94c27

Farrington, N., Kilvington, D., Price, J. and Saeed, A. (2015) *Sport, Racism and Social Media*. London: Routledge.

Feagin, J. and Picca, L.H. (2007) *Two-Faced Racism: Whites in the Backstage and Frontstage*. New York, NY: Routledge.

Gaiser, T.J. and Schreiner, A.E. (2009) *A Guide to Conducting Online Research*. London: Sage Publications.

Gratton, C. and Jones, I. (2010) *Research Methods for Sports Studies* (2nd Edition). London: Routledge.

Hylton, K. (2009) *'Race' and Sport: Critical Race Theory*. London: Routledge.

Hylton, K. and Lawrence, S. (2016) '"For your ears only!" Donald Sterling and backstage racism in sport'. *Ethnic and Racial Studies*, 39 (15): 2740–2757.

Hynes, D. and Cook, A.M. (2013) 'Online belongings: Female fan experiences in online soccer forums'. In Hutchins, B. and Rowe, D. (Eds.) *Digital Media Sport: Technology, Power and Culture in the Network Society*. New York, NY: Routledge, pp. 97–110.

Kilvington, D. (2016) *British Asians, Exclusion and the Football Industry*. London: Routledge.

Kilvington, D. and Price, J. (2017) 'Tackling social media abuse? Critically assessing English football's response to online racism'. *Communication & Sport*. Available at: https://doi.org/10.1177/2167479517745300

Kilvington, D. and Price, J. (2019) 'From backstage to frontstage: Exploring football and the growing problem of online abuse'. In Lawrence, S. and Crawford, G. (Eds.) *Digital Football Cultures Fandom, Identities and Resistance*. London: Routledge, pp. 69–85.

Meyer, R. (2013) '90% of Wikipedia's editors are male – Here's what they're doing about it'. *The Atlantic*, 25 October. Available at: www.theatlantic.com/technology/archive/2013/10/90-of-wikipedias-editors-are-male-heres-what-theyre-doing-about-it/280882/

Moore, N. (2006) *How to Do Research: A Practical Guide to Designing and Managing Research Projects*. London: Facet Publishing.

Reed, M. (2016) *The Research Impact Handbook*. Aberdeenshire: Fast Track Impact.

Walliman, N. (2011) *Your Research Project: Designing and Planning your Work* (3rd Edition). London: Sage Publications.

3

ONLINE RESEARCH ETHICS

As outlined in Chapter 2, the consumption of the internet in nearly every country in the world since the turn of the twenty-first century has provided researchers with greater immediate access to a significant number of people, as well as specific online communities than has been previously the case when adopting more traditional research methods. Despite this Pandora's box of available or potential data to online researchers, however, it is important to retain ethical accountability in our methodological practice. Although online research can be largely faceless, some online projects will engage in a process of face-to-face interaction with the participant, such as through online interviews or online focus groups (possibly through Skype or FaceTime). This has led to a range of ethical issues in online research that need addressing from more traditional ways of collecting and analysing research data, most notably surrounding the process of intrusion, interaction, and invitation with participants (Ruihley and Hardin, 2014).

As a result, there has been the emergence of online research ethics guidelines from universities, academic disciplines, funding organisations, and other external organisations, but there is a lack of an overall consistent framework amongst them. As the Association of Internet Researchers outline in their document *Ethical Decision-Making and Internet Research*, 'no set of guidelines or rules is static; the fields of internet research are dynamic and heterogeneous' (2012: 2). Part of the reason for this is that technological advancement is constantly changing, with new platforms and new ways to communicate emerging at a rapid pace. Naturally, this has implications for online research ethics.

Therefore, the purpose of this chapter is to provide an overview of good research practice surrounding the main ethical considerations when using the internet to collect, analyse, present, and store data. It does this by addressing four main sections, but it will illustrate how there is a clear overlap between them all: (1) the ethical process (including a focus on the methodological process, obtrusive, and non-obtrusive methods, the role of ethics committees and the codes of conduct existing within relevant disciplines and organisations); (2) informed consent (including a focus on informing participants about the aim(s) of the research in an honest and open way that allows them to make an informed choice regarding their participation); (3) harm (including a focus on avoiding deception, the ways in which to protect the identity of the participant, working with vulnerable groups, and protecting the researcher from harm); (4) public versus private platforms (including a focus on the difference between them and the importance of gaining permission from relevant gatekeepers to use platforms or specific sites for the purposes of data collection).

It is also an intention of this chapter to provide a number of rhetorical questions to make you think clearly about the benefits of your proposed or already identified methodology. We offer advice on what principles to think about while recognising the ethical context surrounding your proposed method of online research. This should help you in the individual and group activities selected in this chapter to help guide your learning of ethics and develop good practice in your choice of appropriate online research methods covered in Chapters 4–6 to address your research aim(s) and objectives.

KEY POINTS OF THE CHAPTER

- The ethical process in moving from your research design to collecting, analysing, and disseminating data in order to address your research aim(s) and objectives.
- Understanding the main ethical considerations to address before conducting online research.
- The importance of gaining some form of informed consent (where possible) in online research.
- The importance of the prevention of harm to participants and to the researcher(s) in an online research study.
- Awareness of internet sites used for the collection of data that can be deemed private and those that can be deemed public.

Group activity

- In their analysis of the challenges and ethical approach to engaging with and collecting data from sports fans, Ruihley and Hardin (2014) focus on four major ethical values: Honesty, responsibility, justice, and beneficence. Each of these, they argue, relate to issues of intrusion, interaction, and invitation in an online data collection context. Read this paper and identify some important considerations of good ethical practice surrounding online research that you could adopt in your own practice of online research methods.

The ethical process

Ethics are there to promote good research practice and to act as a safeguard to protect researchers as well as their participants. According to Brancati (2018: 15; emphasis added):

> [R]esearch ethics is a term that refers to the norms, standards, and legal rules regarding appropriate behaviour in the conduct and publication of research. It refers to a range of issues that arise at each stage of the research process and extend beyond concerns for the physical and psychological welfare of human subjects.

As a researcher we have a moral and professional obligation to be ethical in the research we undertake. Thus, compliance with ethical standards is an increasingly vital part of undergraduate, postgraduate, and academic research, a condition of funding from public and private organisations and eligibility to publish in academic books and journals.

This could be the first time you have considered online research ethics to collect data, so it is important to understand the ethical considerations relative to your proposed or ongoing methodological process and how they impact on you as a researcher and your participants. According to the Association of Internet Researchers (2012), ethical decision making can often be complex, with researchers needing to balance the potential benefits of the research with the rights of the participants within the study. As we discussed in Chapter 2, the first major decision that will influence your ethical considerations is your research design: What is or are the research aim(s) and objectives that you want to address around the particular topic area you have chosen to investigate?

As most online research involves the participation of human subjects, there are a range of ethical requirements that you often need to satisfy at a university or organisational level. The ethical process is usually regulated by university ethics committees or within funding organisations. Although there are ethical applications that get approved with no amendments or clarifications needed, the usual practice if you have adhered to ethical principles is that the committee or body might require additional points to satisfy them in their role as overseers of good ethical practice. Once the chair of the ethics committee or lead person at an external research organisation approves the ethics in writing, you are then able to proceed with your strategy of collecting data. However, it is important to remember that ethical considerations occur throughout your research study, beginning at the outset when you design your research aim(s) and objectives around your proposed topic area and acquire ethical approval from the relevant department, institution or external body, to your recruitment of participants and achieving any required access, your methodological approach to the collection of data, how you analyse and disseminate this data and how you manage the storage of data once the research project has been completed.

Depending on your discipline of study within sport studies, there are respective codes of conduct that you should become familiar with when designing your own ethical approach. Some of the more significant ones, for example, include the American Psychological Association, American Sociological Association, Association of Internet Researchers, British Psychological Society, British Sociological Association and, from a more specific sport basis, The British Association of Sport and Exercise Sciences. These organisations are having to continually develop, modify, and refine their own guidelines to advise people of the policy of good ethical online research practice. These are a useful starting point, but if you are comparing them then be aware that there will be some inconsistencies between them, such as around sampling or informed consent. Likewise, it is also good practice to read your own institution's guidelines and, if any funding has been awarded, the codes of conduct often prescribed by the funding body in order to protect their reputation through the adoption of good ethical online research practice.

It will be outlined in Chapter 6 how observational research undertaken online can take different unobtrusive or obtrusive forms, including when the researcher immerses themselves in the group under observation either overtly or covertly and records all the communication taking place between members. This can take the form of creating topics for discussion to discover members' views or simply observe the everyday practice taking place in a natural setting that the researcher is not seeking to disturb in any way. Using netnography as an example here, the level of interaction you are proposing to do with participants in an online community or across a range of online platforms will guide your ethical process. For example, you could simply be undertaking a content analysis of hashtags on Twitter, but you could also be undertaking a deeper thematic analysis of the language contained within the tweets. Or you might decide to do a discussion forum analysis of posters debating a particular issue in a given sport, such as the role of women in leadership positions in a specific governing body, the level of discrimination towards referees in grassroots football or the level of inclusion for disabled people at National Football League matches. Depending on your engagement with participants on certain topics like this, it will naturally dictate the ethical process required to address your research aim(s).

Kozinets (2010) suggests that an open and honest approach to the research aim(s) on certain online sites via a netnographic method could present difficulties for the researcher, with outside interests not always well received by some online communities. This is particularly the case for those groups where very little is known about them, such as far-right groups infiltrating sport or groups of fans associated with sport-related violence. If the intention is to remain covert on the respective website this can create ethical issues, with our duty as researchers scrutinised by an ethics committee or body that will want to know the safeguards in place if you are carrying out some form of covert observation as well as any moral or potential legal issues from undertaking this methodological approach.

Individual activity

- Following on from some initial research ideas you developed from Chapter 2, can you identify any ethical issues that may arise by addressing this topic through research conducted online? If so, how would you go about addressing these to conform to the ethical requirements of your university, workplace, or funding body?

Informed consent

In any research study involving human subjects it is important to gain their informed consent. Gaining consent for more traditional methodologies, such as those that often involve some form of face-to-face interaction, has often been a requirement set by ethics committees or bodies and this can be easily completed by the participant signing some form of informed consent sheet (examples of these are readily available on the internet via widely accessed search engines, but you should also check with your academic institution, workplace, or funding body as they often have standard templates to adopt). Gaining online consent is not always straightforward given that most online projects will involve a faceless process of interaction. However, by engaging in a process of interaction, it can reduce any inhibitions amongst participants and encourage them to consent to giving their opinion, views, and experiences to topics they might not ordinarily comment on, such as racism or homophobia. Indeed, some online research projects will allow participants the opportunity to declare their informed consent, such as through an online survey or an individual or focus group online interview, while it will be more difficult to do in other forms of research, such as on public sites like Twitter.

Good practice, therefore, is to gain some form of recognised consent or provide a document that participants can physically or electronically confirm their participation once they have had sufficient information about the project and the reasons behind why you want them to participate. If this is not possible then you should write something that informs participants that they are giving their consent simply by participating in the research project in some way. For projects using some form of online survey (see Chapter 4), valid consent can be assumed if the questionnaire has been completed although it is good practice to have a check box stating their wish to take part following the information provided as well as a reminder that they are consenting by clicking submit or finish to the survey. For example, in online survey research conducted by one of the authors of this book on sports fans' perceptions and experiences of risk, security, and terrorism at elite sports events, he included the phrase 'by clicking submit you are giving your consent for your anonymous views to be used for research purposes' at the end of the survey (Cleland, 2018).

The delicate nature of the informed consent process on social media is raised by Townsend and Wallace (2017), who note how a user's data can be accessed and analysed without informed consent having been given. In many cases, particularly those using publicly available platforms like Twitter (see the public versus private section later in this chapter), they are unaware of their potential participation in a research study based purely on the things they have said. Indeed, their level of participation may be somewhat different if they knew their language was being observed by a third party (i.e. the researcher). Not surprisingly, the fact that they are unaware that their comments are part of a research study can make their right of withdrawal somewhat complicated (see later in this section). Some researchers might defend the use of this approach as naivety on the part of the social media user, who should have read the terms and conditions of the relevant site to see whether their data can be accessed by a third party who can re-use any data they access. However, this does not make it ethical from the perspective of the researcher (how often do you read the terms and conditions of things you are signing up to?). Thus, consent should be obtained where it cannot be reasonably argued that online data can be considered in the public domain.

It is worth considering, if applicable, for projects involving some form of netnography to ask for the consent of the moderator or administrator of the respective platform or specific site that you want to engage with as to whether you can use it for the collection of data. For some administrators or moderators, simply going on the respective platform with the intention of inviting participants to take part in some research study can be viewed as an ambush or spam and could see you banned immediately, thus cutting you off from a potentially good source of data (Ruihley and Hardin, 2014). In seeking permission, you might need to provide them with an overview of the research study and how the data will be collected and used for your research project in order for them to make an informed choice as to whether to let you proceed. If you are posting on a forum or a discussion board, for example, the moderator or administrator could post a comment to members stating that you have asked for permission to carry out this research project and it has their approval. In this way, the response by online community members is likely to be more receptive to your presence.

If you are engaging in any form of research involving children, then you will need to gain informed consent from their parents or guardian. However, as online research projects often involve a faceless process of the interaction, even if you are not looking to capture data from children how can you be sure that a minor is not conversing on a social media site or completing one of your online surveys? The truth is you cannot, so you would need to devise a methodology that maintains good practice by putting in place a number of safeguards to try and prevent this from happening such as engaging in non-sensitive topics and gaining the appropriate level of informed consent. If you are using online surveys (see Chapter 4), then having an age category of 16 or below also allows you to remove those answers from your sample. It is also good practice to not offer any incentives to participate in your survey, but there are times when participants are incentivised in some way to participate. For example, some professional online survey providers pay a small fee to those who complete one of their surveys, whilst other researchers may place those who participate into a draw to win a prize of some kind.

As outlined in the next section of this chapter, it is good practice to have ethical measures in place that prevent any kind of physical, social, or psychological harm to your participants. Where possible (and in the vast majority of cases unless you can provide some form of ethical defence that you should not disclose your presence for fear of invalidating the data), researchers should *always* disclose their presence, affiliation, and intention behind the research to the online community during any research interaction that takes place at the start of the data collection process. This begins by informing them about the project in a clear and easy to understand way, such as in the form of a participant information sheet or some other means of providing an overview about the project and the benefits or any associated risks regarding their participation in order for them to make an informed choice about whether they consent to voluntarily participate or not (coercion should be avoided). It is important to not over complicate the participant information sheet (examples of these are readily available on the internet via widely accessed search engines, but you should also check with your academic institution, workplace, or funding body as they often have standard templates to adopt) as a lengthy document is unlikely to be read. It should also contain who the researchers are (with some form of contact information should the participant have any questions at *any* stage of the research process), who ethically approved the project (such as a university ethics committee), how the data will be collected, analysed, and disseminated, who has access to the participants' data (the ideal case is as few people as possible), the level of confidentiality provided to participants, and how the data will be stored (with no unauthorised access). When conducting any research with human subjects, it is important to remember that individuals have rights over their personal information, as found with various data protection acts across countries (see the resources section at the end of this chapter), where certain principles need complying with when using and storing personal data.

As well as containing information about the project and why their participation is important and beneficial, it should also detail their right to withdraw (maybe consider installing a set date as to not impact on any eventual dissemination where you publish the results of the study and then one of the participants whose data you have used as an example asks to withdraw). It should also contain measures as to how you or your research collaborators are going to protect the identity of participants. This could take the form of **pseudonyms** (where you use a fictitious name) or any other assignment of some form of identification to them (such as a number).

Research in sport

'"That is like a 24 hours-day tournament!"': Using social media to further an authentic sport experience within sport education', by Luguetti, Goodyear and André (2019).

What was the aim of the research?

The aim of the research was to examine the extent to which social media supports the development of an authentic sport experience within Sport Education (a physical education and sport pedagogical curriculum model designed for use in schools, universities, and community sport clubs). The model has six features (season, competition, score keeping, festivity, team affiliation, and culminating event) and seeks to develop three particular learning outcomes: Competent, literate, and enthusiastic sportspersons by encouraging 'learners to experience the culture of sport and the diverse roles in sport (that extend beyond on a performer)' (p. 79). The researchers present literature that illustrates how social media and digital technologies can accelerate and extend learning within the Sport Education model (in the case of this paper, the players focused on it for 13 weeks), in particular by extending the experience of participants to the culture, values, and ethics of sport.

What was the ethical approach?

This was a mixed method study utilising face-to-face interviews as well as an analysis of a webpage and a private Facebook group that the researchers eventually gained access to. To undertake this, the researchers firstly gained ethical approval from their university ethics committee before any data collection took place. The next phase involved gaining informed consent from the participants for their involvement in the study that involved interviews with the researchers and an analysis of data collected from the webpage.

Although it was not in the initial design of the study, it became clear that Facebook could be used as an additional place where the features of Sport Education could be discussed. By playing for the club for more than two years, the lead researcher had an insider status in examining how female players of a community futsal club in Brazil engaged with the key features of Sport Education through Facebook. In capturing the data from Facebook, initial consent was not sought, but the research team then gained additional consent to access and analyse the players posts.

In reporting the results, pseudonyms were used even though the Facebook group was private, thus limiting the traceability of the participants' identity to individuals external to the study.

What were the key findings?

Players use of Facebook supported the development of an authentic sport experience by strengthening three Sport Education features: Affiliation, festivity, and season. Although the players used Facebook in different ways, the researchers found that the availability to communicate privately as a group on Facebook extended the opportunities for the players to take part in an authentic sport experience through increased opportunities to frequently interact with each other in informal conversations.

Individual activity

- How can you gain informed consent in your methodological approach? If you cannot, what other ways can you think of to make your process of data collection ethical?

Harm

All ethics committees will expect researchers to identify how they are going to address any potential risks of harm to participants as the project moves from design to implementation and then to completion. As researchers we have to put the potential risk of harm or discomfort to participants above our search for any benefits in addressing the research aim(s) we have devised on a particular topic area. As suggested in the previous section, a participant information sheet should inform the participants of their right to withdraw, provide them with sufficient information on how the data will be collected and what it will be used for, where it will be stored, for how long and who has access to it, and guarantee confidentiality in how the results will be disseminated. Where risks to confidentiality are higher, participants should be informed of the nature of the perceived risk to their participation in the research study. In some scenarios, there is also the added importance of protecting vulnerable groups such as children and young people, or those who have some form of impairment from harm if they are going to be our target group for research-related inquiry.

It is important to recognise that harm does not just concern anything physical; it can also include emotional and psychological stress, anxiety, or the potential for some form of humiliation or retribution should the identity of the participant become public. Here, it might be important to consider whether you should publish the results verbatim, particularly if you have acquired any data from what is believed to be a public platform. This can then be led back to the origin of the quote and potentially expose the profile and identity of the participant and the site where the data was captured. Not surprisingly, this can result in some form of repercussion for the participant as it could lead to them being at risk of harm, particularly if they believe that the anonymity and privacy has been breached (Association of Internet Researchers, 2012). Likewise, anonymising secondary data can also be a challenge given the searchable nature of the data stored by some social media companies, so again, good ethical practice is required.

In projects involving some form of netnography (see Chapter 6), the normal approach is for the researcher to interact with the online community in some way, with most studies falling into low levels of risk or harm to the participants. The ethical process can often centre on the nature of the sample and their awareness of their participation in the research study. Are they involuntarily engaging in research without any knowledge that they are (even if the methodological approach is unobtrusive in nature)? Similarly, are they participating involuntarily when the research is obtrusive (for example, it is trying to influence their behaviour in some way)? Both of these approaches will need careful ethical consideration in any ethical application and subsequent approach to the collection of data. According to Kozinets (2010), the downloading of existing posts or archives does not strictly qualify as human subjects research, particularly if the researcher deems the level of risk and identification of the participant to be low; it is only when there is some form of interaction or intervention that he believes consent is needed.

In any online research project involving human participants, deception should be avoided, but there are times where researchers disguise their research aim(s) and intentions by withholding some important information from participants due to concerns about not jeopardising the validity of the study taking place by disclosing themselves to the community under investigation. This can avoid disruption on the online platform as well as any potential harm, but it does, of course, raise ethical concerns and would need appropriate approval before engaging with this type of research method. However, it could be approved by a relevant committee if the participants are not harmed or affected in any way by the research process you have chosen to undertake and you have stated the appropriate benefits by undertaking a particular methodological approach to the collection of data. Moreover, although this chapter primarily focuses on the researcher to participant relationship, it is also important that the researcher puts in place measures to protect their safety also. This could be the threat of violence or some form of physical or psychological harm, to defending yourself against any legal allegations that you have acted inappropriately in the research process.

Individual activity

• Thinking about your own research topic, how could you devise ways to prevent harm to participants and to yourself?

Public versus private data sites

The public versus private source of online data collection is widely debated in the academic research ethics literature (see, for example, Association of Internet Researchers, 2012; British Psychological Society, 2017; Townsend and Wallace, 2017). Not surprisingly, this is often determined by the online platform in question. Consider a public platform like Twitter or more of a private or closed group like those on Facebook. In this way, the data from public platforms presents less ethical issues than those from closed groups or private platforms because of the ease of access to obtaining relevant data. On the other hand, searching for data on platforms that need membership approval or are password protected presents a different type of ethical scenario as these could be argued to be more private and would thus likely need some form of informed consent to obtain and disseminate any data that was collected and analysed.

As expressed by Kozinets (2010: 141), 'Oftentimes the internet is used as a type of textual publishing medium, and culture members are fully aware of this public function'. In line with Walther (2002), publicly available communication online *does* allow for comments to be retrieved, analysed, disseminated, and stored. A key question here is, who 'owns' the data? As suggested earlier, can informed consent be realistically obtained? How are we as researchers going to present the data we collect? Indeed, there is no clear answer to this ambiguous conundrum facing researchers as well as ethics committees. Instead, addressing these questions comes down, to some extent, as to whether it can be reasonably acknowledged that the platform under consideration for research purposes is open to the observation of its content by strangers (British Psychological Society, 2017) or what have been referred to as 'lurkers' (Cleland, Anderson, and Aldridge-Deacon, 2018). For a further description of this see Chapter 6.

An important part of the research process, particularly in terms of obtaining data from an ethical standpoint, is to check the terms, conditions, and guidelines of the respective online platforms that you are engaging with for research purposes. Although this is often directed towards those who use the site to discuss and debate and make some form of text-based contribution, it might also contain information on third parties using the platform to access any data that the site will undoubtedly provide. This could help protect the researcher from any potential legal action should they not follow the terms, conditions, or guidelines appropriately. If you are in any doubt, it is good practice to contact the group administrator or moderator who can advise appropriately. Likewise, you could consider giving the participants the option of opting in or out of the research study (whilst maintaining the ethical practice covered earlier in this chapter surrounding how the data will be collected, analysed, stored, and disseminated). What is important here as a researcher is that you consider the impact of the data on participants and if there is some justification for you to proceed then you need to devise suitable and ethical strategies to protect the participants from as much harm as possible.

Research in sport

'Does race belong on sports blogs? Solidarity and racial discourse in online baseball fan forums', by McGovern (2016).

What was the aim of the research?

The aim of this study was to examine the content and fan discussions across seven baseball blogs hosted in the United States concerning the topic of 'race', ethnicity, and sport for the duration of one calendar year. Selecting just the single sport of baseball to avoid contextual variations, McGovern wanted to analyse the dimensions of each blogging environment and how they influenced discussions of 'race' for evidence of different levels of social solidarity amongst fans engaging with each respective site.

What was the ethical approach?

To examine the discourse taking place, McGovern chose to not seek permission from the administrator of each blog or the online community as she did not want to influence the discourse in any way. McGovern stated that these blogs were in the public domain with content freely available online and membership open to anyone to register as long as they had a valid email address, which she did. Across the seven blogs, McGovern stated that the discussions taking place were not sensitive or private in nature, but she protected each blog and its participants identity by not seeking to collect demographic data as well as using pseudonyms and modified searchable text to further protect the identity of those whose data was captured and presented in the results.

What were the key findings?

Across the calendar year's analysis, McGovern found that bloggers and other participants in the debates taking place rarely discussed 'race'. Instead she found that the baseball blog sites typically discouraged any form of racist discourse, but this was often dependent on the blogging site being examined at that time. For example, on those blogging sites that did not encourage social solidarity, it was outlined how fans were more likely to be aggressive in discussing 'race', whilst on those blogging sites that were more community focused, meaningful discussions about 'race' took place or the online community chose to politely dismiss discussing the topic. Thus, McGovern argues how the social solidarity of an online community can strongly impact on the extent of the racial discourse that takes place.

Individual activity

- Think about the online sites you could potentially utilise to acquire the data you need to address your research aim(s) and objectives. What ethical issues would you face and how could you overcome them?

Conclusion

This chapter has provided an overview of the key ethical considerations researchers need to consider when engaging with online data collected from human participants: Notably the ethical process, informed consent, the prevention of harm, and the public versus private debate surrounding the collection, analysis, dissemination, and storage of data. What the chapter has illustrated is how ethical issues are of paramount importance to the credibility of the research design and safety of the participants as well as the researcher engaging in the research process to disseminate the results in whatever form – such as writing for an undergraduate or postgraduate masters dissertation or PhD or compiling a report for a funding body, or simply writing for publication whether that be a book, chapter, or journal article.

When we think of the world in which the internet operates, particularly social media with the rapid introduction of user-generated content on sites like Facebook, Twitter, Instagram, Snapchat, blogs, or discussion forums, the world of online ethics is problematic. As outlined by the Association of Internet Researchers (2012), internet research guidelines are never static; our process of consuming the internet since the turn of the twenty-first century and subsequent practice of online research is constantly having to change in the fast-moving online world we now operate in. New ethical issues are arising all of the time and it is crucial that researchers maintain good ethical practice in the process of collecting, analysing, disseminating, and storing any data that is collected online. The clear advantages are the immediacy with which data can be captured and analysed, it saves time and resources from more traditional methods, but as this chapter has highlighted it comes with increasing ethical importance.

The result of this is that the internet has become a more frequent method of collecting and analysing data used by researchers across the world. Given this breadth of opportunity across a whole range of discipline areas, there is rarely a simple answer as to the right way to conduct online research ethics. You need to consider all of the associated ethical issues with your approach to online research, particularly given that the continued growth of the internet will result in new contexts, interactions, tools, and opportunities. Responsibility ultimately lies with the researcher and his or her appropriate ethics committee to ensure the implementation of an ethical approach to online research. Each online methodology presents a different set of ethical challenges, but if it is conducted appropriately, the research project is likely to benefit both parties.

SOME IMPORTANT REMINDERS ABOUT ENGAGING IN GOOD ETHICAL PRACTICE ON THE INTERNET

- It is good practice when conducting an ethical application to speak with relevant people at your institution or funding organisation, as well as utilising any resources, ethics guidelines at your respective university, or published work on your proposed methodological framework.
- Ethics do not end at the point of approval by the chair of an ethics committee.
- Make effective use of your supervisor (if appropriate) or research collaborators with any ethical dilemma you face.
- Where possible, always gain some form of informed consent from participants.
- It is good practice to contact the group administrator or moderator of discussion boards or forums to ask for access to potential participants.
- Consideration needs to be given whether to paraphrase quotes or to report them verbatim when writing up your findings.
- Researchers need to balance the potential benefits of the project with the rights of the participants.

Important resources

- Association of Internet Researchers – https://aoir.org/reports/ethics2.pdf
- British Psychological Society – www.bps.org.uk/news-and-policy/ethics-guidelines-internet-mediated-research-2017
- Data Protection in the United Kingdom – www.gov.uk/data-protection
- EU General Data Protection Regulation (GDPR) – https://eugdpr.org/

References

Association of Internet Researchers (2012) 'Ethical decision-making and internet research'. Available at: https://aoir.org/reports/ethics2.pdf

Brancati, D. (2018) *Social Scientific Research*. London: Sage Publications.

British Psychological Society (2017) 'Ethics guidelines for internet-mediated research'. Available at: www.bps.org.uk/news-and-policy/ethics-guidelines-internet-mediated-research-2017

Cleland, J. (2018) 'Sports fandom in the risk society: Analyzing perceptions and experiences of risk, security and terrorism at elite sports events'. *Sociology of Sport Journal*. Available via OnlineFirst at: https://journals.humankinetics.com/doi/abs/10.1123/ssj.2018-0039

Cleland, J., Anderson, C. and Aldridge-Deacon, J. (2018) 'Islamophobia, war and non-Muslims as victims: An analysis of online discourse on an English Defence League message board'. *Ethnic and Racial Studies*, 41 (9): 1541–1557.

Kozinets, R. (2010) *Netnography: Doing Ethnographic Research Online*. London: Sage Publications.

Luguetti, C., Goodyear, V.A. and André, M.H. (2019) "That is like a 24 hours-day tournament!" Using social media to further an authentic sport experience within sport education'. *Sport, Education and Society*, 24 (1): 78–91.

McGovern, J. (2016) 'Does race belong on sports blogs? Solidarity and racial discourse in online baseball fan forums'. *Communication & Sport*, 4 (3): 331–346.

Ruihley, B.J. and Hardin, R. (2014) 'Sport fans and online data collection: Challenges and ethics'. *Journal of Applied Sport Management*, 6 (3): 1–15.

Townsend, L. and Wallace, C. (2017) 'The ethics of using social media data in research: A new framework'. In Woodfield, K. (Ed.) *The Ethics of Online Research (Advances in Research Ethics and Integrity, Volume 2)*. Bingley: Emerald Publishing Limited, pp. 189–207.

Walther, J.B. (2002) 'Research ethics in internet-enabled research: Human subjects issues and methodological myopia'. *Ethics and Information Technology*, 4 (3): 205–216.

4

ONLINE SURVEYS

A questionnaire survey is a tool used by researchers to capture qualitative and quantitative data from participants that measures their views, experience, behaviour and knowledge on a particular research topic. As suggested by Murray (2014: 3), 'using surveys in research is an effective way of gathering certain types of factual and descriptive information in a systematic and structured way'. Traditional methods of surveying comprised telephone interviewing, self-administered questionnaires, or conducted through face-to-face surveys, such as the approach taken by those market researchers you often see in public venues (such as city centres or public transport locations). Although these remain part of survey data collection, two common types of online surveying have emerged as an alternative methodological approach that can save time and costs over more traditional survey-based methods: (1) email; and (2) web-based. Given the opportunities created by the internet to conduct online survey research, the challenge for researchers is to use online surveys in the most effective way to address their research aim(s) and objectives.

This chapter centres on five main sections that illustrate the challenges and opportunities for researchers working in this growing field of empirical enquiry: (1) planning and developing an online survey (illustrating the stages through which an online survey will take place, as well as the advantages and disadvantages of conducting an email or web-based survey); (2) sampling (focusing on probability and non-probability sampling techniques); (3) online survey research questions (examining the use of closed and open-ended questions and the overall structure of the survey); (4) conducting an online survey (devising strategies to maximise the number of completions, including good practice through the use of a pilot study to detect any unforeseen errors); and (5) under coverage and non-responses on an online survey (focusing on maintaining reliability and validity and being aware of some of the issues that could arise throughout the duration of the project).

As with the other chapters in this book, there will be questions throughout the chapter addressing all aspects of the online survey process to help inform your own knowledge. The chapter will also address a number of ethical issues that occur throughout the online survey data collection and analysis process, in particular focusing on the importance of a participant information sheet at the start of the survey that provides an overview of the study so that an informed choice can be made by potential participants as to whether to consent to participate or not, their importance in contributing to your research aim(s) and objectives, who the researchers are and how their data will be collected, analysed, disseminated, and stored, including the protection of all personal data through anonymity and confidentiality (see Chapter 3 for more details on this aspect of the research process).

KEY POINTS OF THE CHAPTER

- Planning and developing an online survey to address the research aim(s) and objectives.
- Identify the advantages and disadvantages of conducting an online survey.
- Designing questions and conducting an online survey.
- Understand the methods employed in administering an online survey.
- Understand the difference between probability and non-probability sampling techniques to recruit participants when using an online survey.
- Recognise the reasons behind coverage errors and non-responses in an online survey.
- Reflect on the ethical process when conducting an online survey.

Planning and developing an online survey

For research projects utilising an online survey as either the sole methodology or part of a multi-method approach, planning is an important component of delivering a successful outcome that effectively addresses the research aim(s) and objectives. Fundamentally, in the planning and developing phase you have some control over the survey, but once it is distributed on the internet this is somewhat lost as there are times when the internet allows for material to be widely circulated without the researcher's control, such as on social media sites like Twitter where original tweets can be retweeted numerous times. Thus, the decisions that you make in the planning and development phase are crucial and will have a strong impact on the validity and reliability of your data once the survey is released and the collection of data begins.

Part of this is recognising that online survey research is a process, often consisting of six important phases, with each phase impacting on the next: (1) establishing the research aim(s) and objectives (what do you want to find out and why); (2) devising a sampling frame (probability or non-probability); (3) developing the survey (choosing the survey platform; writing the questions; piloting the survey); (4) collecting the data (monitoring the number and quality of responses); (5) analysing the data (either through methods of quantitative and/or qualitative analysis); and (6) presenting the results (via assignments, dissertations, projects, reports, or any other form of publication).

If you are planning to use an email survey to address your research aim(s) and objectives, the survey is either contained within the body of the email message or sent via an attachment into a participant's inbox for them to complete and then reply to the original email sender with their response. In a web-based survey, this is often distributed on specific websites for potential respondents to initially see the link and decide whether to complete the survey. Indeed, both forms of online surveying require the participant to self-select (i.e. they freely choose themselves) as to whether to go ahead and participate in the research project. One advantage of an email or web-based survey is that participants can complete it in their own time at their own choice of location as long as they have internet access – whether that be via their smartphone on a bus or train, at the gym, or via a tablet or computer at their workplace, home, or place of study. What this does is allow the participants to give the email or web-based survey their full attention (questions can be re-read, for example) as there is no real time pressure in which to complete it (such as via a face-to-face or telephone questionnaire survey, or interview) as the survey remains live 24 hours a day, seven days a week, until the end date set by the researcher.

A separate advantage of web-based surveys in comparison to email surveys is that they are not restricted to any mailing lists to distribute the link to the survey, like the email addresses of students and staff at certain universities or at a sporting organisation. Instead, depending on your method of distribution it could be open to a significant number of potential participants based on their locality, club, or their role in certain sports, such as coaches in swimming or gymnastics, referees in cricket or rugby, or fans in football or basketball. The aim is simply to capture a range of views (web-based surveys are good for sensitive topics in comparison to email surveys where anonymity is lost through knowledge of the participant's email address), but this is dependent on your method of survey distribution. Indeed, web-based surveys can also be beneficial in those research studies that examine specific groups or closed populations of people. For example, in research by Cleland, O'Gorman and Webb (2018), the assistance provided by an institutional gatekeeper (in the case of this article it was the English Football Association) in distributing an online survey through their networks into County Football Associations helped them gain the views of over 2,000 football (mainly grassroots) referees to a project that examined their experience of officiating since the launch of a Respect campaign that was introduced in 2008 to stop them from leaving the game as a result of the poor behaviour of individuals (players, coaches, spectators, and parents) and teams. This impact research subsequently shaped public debate via the British mainstream media and has helped lead to pressure being put on the English Football Association to try new policy initiatives in aiding the matchday experience for grassroots referees.

Group activity

• What are the advantages and disadvantages of conducting an email or web-based self-selecting survey?

Sampling

As stated at the outset of this chapter, as researchers we are often interested in measuring the attitudes, behaviours, experiences, and knowledge of our participants on certain topics and, because of this, we tend to have a specific population or group of people in mind who we want to participate. We do this by engaging in a sampling frame that is either **probability** or **non-probability.** If you adopt appropriate **probability** sampling techniques, you can make more valid inferences about a population as each member of the population has an equal probability of being chosen for the sample due to its random selection of participants (i.e. it is representative of the population and ensures the validity of statistical conclusions). With **non-probability** sampling, we cannot be sure that all individuals in the population have an equal chance of being chosen so we cannot generalise to the population.

According to Sue and Ritter (2012a: 2), 'a population is the entire group of individuals, groups, or objects to which you would like to generalise your research results – for example, citizens of a country, students at a university, or employees of a company. When you collect data on every member of a population, you are conducting a census'. But this approach is not always feasible or practical particularly given the inconsistencies in internet access amongst populations of people across the world (as a reminder, in Chapter 1 we detailed that as of January 2019 the world's population was 7.7 billion, with nearly 4.4 billion internet users). Once you identify a population, the next task is to find or generate a list of population members – referred to as a sampling frame. Some easily accessible probability ones that you could utilise (with appropriate ethical permission) include email lists of students or staff at a specific university or members of an organisation. If this is your methodological approach, then you are ready to draw your sample and select those to participate in the research through either a random sample; a systematic random sample; a stratified sample; or a cluster sample (see Chapter 2 for a fuller description of these sampling methods).

Some characteristics of **non-probability** sampling techniques in an online survey are **convenience, self-selection,** and **snowball** (see Chapter 2 for a full description of these sampling methods). For some sport-related research projects, probability sampling is not of prime importance; instead the potential for large numbers of respondents are deemed by some researchers to be more valuable in addressing the research aim(s) and objectives. In snowball sampling, the recruitment of future participants is made by existing ones who refer them to the researcher as a result of their own social networks and contacts (both online and offline). This is often an important process in small populations with people knowing each other or those in highly targeted populations and this sampling approach can help make the data more valid and reliable.

For those online surveys more exploratory in nature, then a convenience sample might be the appropriate sampling technique to use. Convenience sampling involves a non-systematic approach that allows participants to self-select into the sample. It often requires less time and effort than probability sampling if the survey is likely to generate a significant number of completions, but statistical inference to a wider population is problematic because any form of self-selection by participants is not representative of any underlying population as those completing the survey are more than likely to have an interest in the topic area being researched. In convenience sampling there is no restriction to their participation, and it only ends if the researcher sets a date when the survey will close. By adopting this approach, the survey is likely to be distributed in specific online communities, discussion forums, and chat rooms as well as on social media accounts, to gain the attention of people browsing or corresponding with the relevant site. In some cases, the onus is on the researcher to promote the research topic in as many sites as they can to try and increase the number of responses, but this does not apply to every online survey project as each will have different aims and objectives.

However, as we illustrated in Chapter 3, this can also be viewed as a violation of privacy by some members of these sites being targeted by researchers. Thus, it is important to seek the permission of moderators or administrators of online platforms, where possible (sometimes referred to as gatekeepers), to collect data from the online community through an online survey. We are talking about more specific sites like a sport or club forum, rather than social media sites like Facebook or Twitter, but cooperation can be crucial to the success of any research study in terms of responses and the amount of data being collected, particularly if the administrator or moderator approves your presence on the website as a researcher and shows their support of the project, such as by writing a supportive post for the attention of the online community.

Research in sport

'"Nothing will be the same again after the Stade de France attack": Reflections of association football fans on terrorism, security, and surveillance', by Cleland and Cashmore (2018).

What was the aim of the research?

Following the attempted terrorist attack on the Stade de France on 13 November 2015, during a game between France and Germany, Cleland and Cashmore asked 1,500 association football fans, via an online survey, to reflect on their own experiences of security and surveillance when attending matches and how they felt the attempted terrorist attack would impact on the management of football crowds in the future.

What were the methods used?

Given their use of online surveys to address a range of social issues in sport, particularly football, the article states how Cleland and Cashmore have built up relationships with over 150 moderators and administrators of football forums, who give their permission for the inclusion of links to online surveys as part of a post on the specific forum that provides an overview of the topic and why the participation of the particular online community is important to address the research aim(s) and objectives. This is part of their approach to tackling any ethical issues in online surveys, where good practice is also stipulated through participant anonymity and ways to prevent harm. In terms of the survey's construction, it contained a range of closed and open-ended questions in order for fans to provide an honest reflection of their views towards terrorism, security, and increasing surveillance at football matches. Closed questions centred on general demographic information like sex, age, and the club they supported as well as whether it was inevitable football would be a target for terrorism. Open-ended questions asked participants how football fans can help the police and security services and what they think will change post-Paris in terms of crowd management at elite football matches.

What were the key findings?

Drawing on the theoretical framework of Michel Foucault to illustrate the growing impact of security and surveillance on the matchday experience of football fans, the results outlined how some fans accepted the need for additional measures of security in order to protect their safety, but other fans resisted this by arguing it was overly excessive and intrusive and it would negatively affect their matchday experience. The majority of fans (84 percent) were clear that it was inevitable that the global profile of football makes it a target for terrorism with 82 percent stating how fans can help assist the police and security services by being complicit to their requests concerning increased security checks entering the stadium, being vigilant, and reporting any suspicious behaviour. The article concludes by suggesting that given the global focus on sports like football, and the increasing threat levels of events where thousands of people congregate in one place, fans are only likely to encounter even greater security and surveillance measures in the future. This, Cleland and Cashmore argue, will be the new norm when attending elite level sporting events, such as football matches.

A common question often asked by students and researchers with regards to conducting an online survey is what are an appropriate number of responses to collect. Fundamentally, there is no golden rule, as the two 'research in sport' case studies used in the chapter illustrate (as a reminder, one collected 1,500 responses and the other collected 70 responses and both were published in academic journals). Likewise, some academics have published books on a handful of qualitative interviews and there are others that have published books based on data collected from hundreds of participants. You are best to liaise with your supervisor or research collaborator(s) and set a time frame to collect data and then review its quality before deciding if you have reached what is termed **data saturation** and can use the data you have already collected to address your research aim(s) and objectives. In non-probability sampling, the number is always open to debate because in some cases time and cost constraints as well as the topic area being examined can lead to the selection of a smaller sample. It is the view of the authors of this book that whilst those surveys adopting a non-probability sampling technique are not representative of the general population, they are useful in obtaining a sample of a specific population to better gain some insight on a topic area (particularly those that are under-researched) rather than no insight taking place at all.

Group activity

- A lot of sport-related online surveys will adopt a non-probability sampling technique. What are the advantages and disadvantages of using this sampling technique to collect data in an online survey?

Online survey questions

Designing and constructing an online survey is a difficult and complex task. In terms of the actual design, the survey's visual presentation (including the background, text, colour, and font size) is an important element not to be underestimated. You might want to consider having the logo of the university you are studying at or are employed at or consider using another suitable background, such as a sports field or something similar depending on the focus of your research topic. As we outlined in Chapter 3, a welcome screen detailing a participant information sheet is required to provide a background to the study and why their participation is important, the estimated time it is likely to take to complete the survey, all the relevant ethical issues that you have considered and addressed, and the contact information of the main researcher. It is also courteous to include a thank you note at the end of the survey when the participant has clicked on submit or finish to end the online survey.

The most effective online surveys stick to their research aim(s), are unambiguous, and capture the interest of participants (Sue and Ritter, 2012b). In online surveys, the first question is often the most important because it eases the participant into the line of questioning. As they go through the survey the participant hopefully starts to become more invested in it and are then less likely to not submit their response. Too much information and complex instructions across the survey can consequently lead to participant frustration that results in partial completions, missing data (non-response), or both. Sometimes shorter surveys can provide the researcher with a greater amount of quality data, but there is often a need for an online survey to involve a number of pages as to not overcrowd a single survey page with too much information and questions.

Individual activity

- Pick one of the research topic areas below and think of a suitable first question to capture the attention of participants who are interested in your online survey. Test this out with other people to see what they think.

  - Under coverage of women's sport in the print media.
  - The rise in online sports gambling.
  - The changing nature of policing at football matches.
  - The use of performance enhancing drugs in amateur rugby.
  - The dominance of white people in leadership positions in sport governing bodies.
  - The lack of funding provided to grassroots sport.
  - The physical and emotional abuse directed towards grassroots sports officials.

Some research projects will already have a theoretical framework in which to underpin the online survey questions, but for others the data that they collect will devise the appropriate theoretical framework to help contextualise the results. Therefore, one of the most important aspects of any survey are the questions being asked to participants. In the case of an online survey, you need to choose whether they are they going to be mainly **closed**, mainly **open,** or a mixture of both?

In **closed** questions, respondents often choose one answer from a restricted number of alternative options. These could include a simple 'yes' or 'no' or 'true' or 'false' response or include other check boxes (such as asking the participant to 'select all that apply' or only being able to 'choose one answer' from a select list of options) to more Likert responses that measure agreement or disagreement to a question or statement with options such as: 'strongly agree'; 'agree;' 'neither agree or disagree'; 'disagree'; 'strongly disagree'. It is also advisable to have alternative options like 'don't know', 'not applicable', or 'prefer not to disclose' on certain questions as your participants might not have a clear view one way or the other if asked to respond with either a 'yes' or 'no'. A benefit of including closed questions is the ease with which to analyse this type of data once the online survey has been completed. They can also include particular demographic questions including sex, ethnicity, age, location, income, or occupation that are often located at the end of online surveys (but not exclusively so). As outlined in Chapter 3, the use of demographic data helps combat the anonymity of the participant by allowing the researcher to still state the sex, ethnicity, age bracket and potential location, sports role, club they support, or level of refereeing of the participant without breaching any form of confidentiality in their writing up of the results.

Open questions allow participants to answer in their own words in an empty single or multi-line text box. The size of the text box is important because it illustrates to the participant the kind of length of response you would like them to provide (it is then up to them whether to provide no response, a minimal response, or a lengthy response). Open-ended questions can provide more validity than closed questions because they are not just responding in some way to a list of closed responses created by the researcher. It is good practice to not employ too many open-ended questions in an online survey because participants can be frustrated at this, but instead to use them to gain a deeper insight on particular issues relevant to your research objectives. This might include the use of hyperlinks that subsequently allow the participant to read an additional article, such as an online newspaper article or relevant online report, that is embedded within a question to get some deeper context as to what the question is asking. Although some participants will naturally provide a lot of detail in an open-ended text box if they are engaged with the topic area, be aware that others will skip open-ended questions as they want to get to the end of the survey as quickly as possible.

EXAMPLES OF OPEN-ENDED QUESTIONS

- What strategies can we implement to more effectively tackle racism in football?
- Evidence has suggested that there is a lack of women in leadership positions at sports governing bodies. What is your opinion on some of the reasons behind this?
- In what ways could governing bodies make the experience of officiating better for referees?
- In what ways can we encourage children to maintain a healthy lifestyle?

In any online survey design you might choose to include what are often referred to as **skip pattern** questions; questions that are invisible to the participant who is unaware that they are being directed to a new set of questions based on an answer they have provided – such as sex, occupation, or their role at an organisation or within a specific sport (for example, fan, player, coach, parent, referee, administrator). In an online survey this means that they are not forced to read and answer unnecessary questions and, in doing so, can improve the validity of the survey by eliminating the possibility of illogical answers from participants (such as men commenting on questions meant for women and vice versa). This is definitely an advantage of online surveys as traditional paper surveys can confuse participants with some of their instructions to skip a set of questions if the participant does not meet criteria to continue in the logical order (for example, questions that say 'if no, please go to question 5', when the participant has just addressed question 2). Online surveys avoid this and is one reason why there are sometimes more errors contained within traditional paper surveys. This means that some traditional paper surveys require greater levels of editing by researchers, which can be time intensive.

Research in sport

'Influences on parental involvement in youth sport', by Knight et al. (2016).

What was the aim of the research?

Focusing on the widely researched area of parental involvement in youth sport, the study had two research aims: (1) what are the individual and environmental influences on parental involvement; and (2) how is parental involvement influenced by these individual and environmental factors?

What were the methods used?

To address the two research aims, once ethical approval had been provided, the researchers focused on the United States (USA) and the United Kingdom (UK) to capture their data. In the USA, emails were sent to 46 league directors explaining the study and seeking permission to contact the parents of athletes on teams affiliated to their respective league. Once permission had been acquired, emails were then sent to parents containing an overview of the project and a link to the online survey. In the UK, coaches and club managers known to some of the researchers were contacted and provided with an overview of the study before being asked to forward an email to parents containing an overview of the study and a link to the online survey. The survey was distributed via the Qualtrics survey software and contained a total of 34 questions (15 closed and 19 open), with an additional 15 questions depending on their response to previous questions in the survey. Questions were grouped into five categories based on existing literature on the research topic area: (1) general demographic information such as age, marital status, number of children; (2) the parents own experiences of sport; (3) what the parents wanted the experience of sport to be for their child(ren); (4) the perception of parents towards their involvement in their child(ren)'s sport; and (5) the perception of parents of influences on their involvement in their child(ren)'s sport. After an initial pilot study, a total of 70 parents completed the online survey. The researchers justified the use of an online survey by stressing the importance of parents avoiding social desirability by being true and honest as to the individual and environmental influences on their involvement in youth sport.

What were the key findings?

The main finding was that the involvement of parents in sport is influenced by a range of individual and environmental factors. Parents often reflected on their own past experiences of sport and stressed the need for their child(ren) to have a positive experience of participating in sport, yet were also concerned about the overly competitive nature with which youth sport can operate, such as pressure from coaches and parents (themselves included). Parents expressed some difference in wanting to be involved in their child(ren)'s sport, with the researchers calling for sport organisations, practitioners, and coaches to be aware of the different attitudes parents have with regards to their varied involvement in youth sport when devising new policy initiatives to implement in youth sport. Concluding the study, the researchers outline the need for parents to not be treated as a homogenous group, but instead recognise that each of them will have different experiences and will be seeking different outcomes for their child(ren) in participating in youth sport.

Group activities

- What are the opportunities and challenges of using open-ended questions in online survey research?
- Discuss how open and closed-ended survey questions can complement each other.

Once the response to the survey has been submitted by the participant, it is stored electronically and collated for the researcher on whatever electronic survey platform they are using for its development and distribution. An advantage of this is the direct processing of data in its electronic form as it bypasses the time-consuming process and potential of manual errors involved in editing, coding, and other checks required in more traditional paper-based methods. It also offers advanced methods for confidentiality as there is greater security in storing the data than more traditional forms of survey research where face-to-face contact or some form of interaction between the researcher and the participant took place.

Depending on the platform you use to construct and distribute the online survey, it will also likely have a feature that helps process the data in an analytical context, including simple **descriptive statistics** or the potential for **cross-tabulations** of the data captured from the closed questions. For example, **descriptive statistics** describe the basic features of the results by providing a statistical summary of individual questions on the online survey, whilst **cross-tabulations** analyse the relationship between multiple variables to understand the correlations between different variables in the results – such as demographic data like sex and the answers to one specific closed question. Most software used in an online survey allows researchers to create cross-tabulation tables that are displayed in rows and columns. This makes it easy to visually compare, for example, males compared to females and how they responded to certain closed questions.

Not surprisingly, for the open-ended data, manual coding of large datasets can be time consuming and there are software packages available to help with this process, such as NVivo for more qualitative answers that picks out unique words or phrases stipulated by the researcher. Depending on the size of data you have collected and your strategy for analysing the raw data, a different option could involve the researcher or research team manually analysing the open-ended responses themselves to identify recurring themes within the data. This would give you good experience of working with real-life data and the process of coding involved in developing themes to explain your qualitative results (for more detail on analysing data see Chapter 7).

SEVEN KEY POINTS WHEN DESIGNING ONLINE SURVEY QUESTIONS

1) The questions should always address your research aim(s) and objectives.
2) Some questions require instructions for the participant to follow, including:

- select one option only
- select all that apply
- rank the following answers from 1 to 6 which 1 being the most important and 6 the least important

3) Avoid jargon and write questions that participants will easily understand.
4) Write short, concise questions as non-responses will increase with longer questions and longer surveys.
5) Be sure that the survey is meaningful to those participants you are targeting through your sampling frame.
6) Avoid leading questions that could be argued to direct participants to a particular answer.
7) Avoid too many open-ended questions in order to prevent the participant feeling a sense of frustration in requiring their constant opinion. Remember they are giving their time voluntarily.

Conducting an online survey

Before distributing your online survey to your target group or subset of the population, it is important to adopt good practice through a pilot study with a small sample (Vicente and Reis, 2011). Fundamentally, this process helps with validity and reliability by providing valuable feedback that could raise an important element of question misinterpretation back to you as the researcher to make any necessary changes before wider distribution. For example, you might ask yourself why participants are not answering a particular question or are providing very short or illogical answers to what you intended the question to address. If you did not engage in pilot research and realise that the survey contains some errors when it has been widely distributed, then this could lead to you having to release the survey again but to different participants. If this was the case, then it would be a waste of your initial time.

Not surprisingly, the recruitment of participants is crucial for a good response rate – people are busy with various demands on their time – so it is important that you consider your target audience and give thought to some important components of online survey research – namely, the initial contact, potential follow-up messages, and whether any incentives to complete the survey will be offered. Fundamentally, you need to get the attention of potential participants in any initial contact via email or on the internet when trying to advertise your web-based survey. In the best-case scenario, once you distribute the online survey, the responses come back with a good level of detail in the time frame you set out to collect the data. However, best-case scenarios are often a challenge and follow-up contact is often needed. The secret is to be versatile with your approach and give yourself enough time to react if the best-case scenario does not happen for whatever reason. Even if your initial plans change with the distribution of the survey, be mindful that an advantage of online surveys is the speed with which data can be collected and analysed. Thus, if your time management of conducting the survey has flexibility built in, then you could leave the survey open for a longer period of time or you could possibly try other relevant sites on the internet to gain more completions. In some circumstances an incentive might be offered for their participation (a voucher can be posted to their address or printed out as a coupon or the respondent is given their reward when they log on to a website and enter a particular code). Another strategy is to offer nonmaterial incentives, such as providing a summary of the survey results to any site or group you made contact with once the research has been completed.

Individual activity

- Put yourself in the position of a potential participant thinking about completing your online survey – what elements of good online survey practice could tempt them to complete it for you?

After the data collection period has ended, Benfield and Szlemko (2006) outline how the data should be 'cleaned' to potentially eliminate incomplete, incorrect, or illogical answers, and those participants who are just taking part to ruin the results (for example, those who write their age as 130 or purposely write responses to open-ended questions that illustrate they have no interest in what the true meaning of the question was asking). However, it is important that you do not just dismiss answers that do not support your research aim(s). For those research projects that do not have an initial hypothesis, your data might illustrate a different meaning to what you might have expected and as researchers we should always be guided by what the data is showing with that particular group of participants, not what we think or expect it to show (see Chapter 7 for an analysis of emerging codes and patterns within data).

Depending on your level of experience and budget you may decide to employ a commercial web-based survey organisation to conduct the research on your behalf by generating a list of potential participants that match your sampling frame. However, we would advise you trying to undertake this yourself, particularly given the platforms you could utilise (SurveyMonkey, Google Surveys, SurveyHero, Qualtrics, and Online Surveys (formerly called Bristol Online Survey) being just five that you to could consider – see website links at the end of this chapter, but also check to see what online survey tools your place of study or workplace subscribe to). The advantage of this approach is that you do not have to launch the survey until you are absolutely ready to do so and you have gone through the appropriate checks, such as with your supervisor or research collaborator(s) and with a small number of participants as part of a pilot study to test its presentation, structure, and quality and coherence of questions in addressing your research aim(s) and objectives.

Coverage error and non-response

When undertaking an online survey, you need to be aware of issues that can impact on its validity and reliability. Under coverage, a lack of suitable sample frameworks, and non-responses are likely to have the most detrimental impact on online surveys. As illustrated by Vicente and Reis (2011), under coverage makes the internet an inadequate tool in which to make valid inferences, particularly on opinion polling and attitude surveys. Yes, free internet access in public libraries can increase the opportunities for those groups in society who cannot afford the subscription costs or have access to a smartphone, but the difference this will make will be marginal. Remember that in Chapter 1 and in earlier in this chapter we referred to 3.3 billion of the world's population (out of 7.7 billion as of January 2019) that do not access the internet (some of which we recognise will be children).

In terms of non-response, one reason behind this is that potential participants may look at the construction of the survey and decide not to participate because of concerns they might have surrounding security and privacy. By providing an overview of the ethical diligence of your online survey in a participant information sheet it can encourage respondents to give less socially desirable answers and, in doing so, aid the data's accuracy. For those researchers who send their survey out via email, one problem could be that it could get lost in a participant's inbox if they decide to not complete the survey immediately and then forget about it (Vicente and Reis, 2011). In scenarios like this, it is best to be aware of the number of responses you are receiving and if they are not coming in as quickly as you had hoped, then you might need to send a reminder out to participants within a week or so. The same approach might also be needed for web-based surveys as you are likely to attract new respondents if you send a reminder message out to a specific site or across multiple sites on the internet that the survey remains open for participants to take part as they are likely to see it for the first time (they might not have been online when you initially distributed it).

Other factors that could result in a non-response or partially answered online surveys is through poor presentation and the wording of questions that can make it difficult for the participant to understand or that the questions de-motivate them in some way (possibly due to the length of an individual question or the length of the overall survey). As well as making sure the online survey is well designed, informative, engaging, and appropriately structured before you distribute it, some ways to pre-empt non-responses include the importance of appealing to the self-interest of participants in the participant information sheet and to get your sampling frame right (as illustrated earlier in the chapter). Here, you need to state the importance of the topic area and seek to influence those who do not have an opinion to not take part, instead of them providing partial or illogical answers to questions in your online survey.

Group activity

- What strategies can be put in place to reduce under coverage and non-responses in an online survey?

Given there are no interviewers physically present in an online survey, the self-administered nature of access and completion could lead to higher levels of non-response and errors in answering questions. However, be assured that no other method is 100 percent perfect – each will also have various problems to consider – so, as long as you adopt good practice, most problems could be somewhat negated. As a researcher you also need to be aware of participants who might be trying to complete the survey more than once, particularly on those surveys that offer some kind of incentive to participate, such as a shopping voucher or a chance to win a prize. In circumstances like this, there are some techniques you might want to consider, such as checking the data for incorrect, incomplete, irrelevant, or inaccurate responses and subsequently correcting or removing it (what we referred to earlier as **data cleaning**) or whether the software you are using allows you to see the recipient's internet protocol address (often listed as an **IP address**).

Other errors to be aware of are the participants giving socially desirable answers – giving what they believe to be the 'right' answer because they want to conform to social norms. This is more of an issue in face-to-face research as online surveys tend to lead to more honest accounts because they involve no actual interaction with a researcher. But online surveys are not immune to this, so remind the participant in the participant information sheet that their response will be treated as anonymous and confidential as this should, at least, reduce the possibility of this occurring.

ADVANTAGES OF ONLINE SURVEYS

- Immediate access to a large number of potential respondents across a wide geographical area.
- Can collect a lot of quantitative and qualitative data through a mix of closed and open-ended questions in a relatively short period of time.
- Low costs – no need to pay for printing and mail.
- Can be launched quickly, particularly on topical areas.
- Allows for multimedia use (images and audio) as well as hyperlinks to material (such as newspaper stories, reports, or additional points) that the participant can engage with before writing their response.
- Direct data entry to the survey platform to aid the analytical process.
- Skip patterns on questions should they be needed.
- Participants can complete the survey in their own time at their choice of location, with limited researcher influence.
- Ethical considerations such as a description of the project, researcher contact details, informed consent, anonymity, and confidentiality can be built into a participant information sheet at the start of the online survey (see Chapter 3).

DISADVANTAGES OF ONLINE SURVEYS

- The potential for poor quality data if the survey is not planned and designed effectively.
- Lacking in potential of inference to the target population of the survey if you are adopting a non-probability sampling technique.
- Potential reliance on software to design and distribute the online survey and analyse the data.
- A lack of control once the survey is distributed on the internet. Thus, you are unaware who is responding to your online survey.
- The process of self-selection for email and web-based surveys.
- The potential for under coverage, non-responses, and illogical answers.

Conclusion

The growth and potential of the internet has changed the process of engagement, data collection, and analysis for researchers utilising online surveys to address their research aim(s) and objectives. In addressing this type of research method, this chapter has focused on five key sections that researchers need to consider when conducting an online survey: Planning and developing; sampling; establishing online survey questions; conducting the survey; and devising ways to reduce coverage error and non-response. Across the chapter we have provided examples as to how the internet has provided greater opportunities to conduct online survey-related research, but it also has provided many challenges that researchers need to be aware of and address in their research methodology. Some of these include being aware of non-responses, a lack of suitable sampling frames, data quality and coverage; each of which can have a detrimental impact on the success of an online survey effectively addressing the original research aim(s).

Some advantages of conducting an online survey are the potential global reach to your sample size and the speed with which data can be collected and analysed by survey software, thus saving researchers considerable time and cost than is the case with more traditional face-to-face or postal surveys. The results of online surveys can be available for analysis in a matter of days or weeks, rather than via traditional methods which can be some months away from being finalised. The advancements in technology also allow for the inclusion of multimedia tools (such as video and audio) as well as the use of hyperlinks that help inform the participant ahead of them completing certain closed and open-ended questions.

Finally, despite the focus of this chapter, when you are considering your methodological options, sometimes an online survey might not always be the best choice. If, for example, your geographic area for the focus of data collection is small, then telephone, Skype, or even face-to-face interviews, or more traditional paper surveys might be a better alternative and could provide you with better quality data than an online survey might do as you are more in control of the data collection process. This could provide greater validity to your study and increase your response rate whilst reducing any non-response errors that might occur through an online survey.

SOME IMPORTANT REMINDERS WHEN USING AN ONLINE SURVEY TO ADDRESS YOUR RESEARCH AIM(S) AND OBJECTIVES

- A key part of conducting your online survey is the sampling frame you are adopting.
- Probability sampling often occurs through a random sample; a systematic random sample; a stratified sample; a multistage sample; or a cluster sample.
- Non-probability sampling often occurs through a convenience, self-selection, and snowball sample.
- Align your closed and/or open-ended questions to your research aims(s) and objectives when constructing an online survey. It is easy to try and collect a broad range of data, but this could frustrate participants and result in them abandoning the survey before it is completed.
- It is advisable on some closed questions where the participant is asked to express and opinion to also include some options like 'don't know', 'not applicable', or 'prefer not to disclose' so they are not always forced to choose, for example between 'yes' or 'no'.
- The first question on any online survey is crucial to capture the attention of a participant. One that is too complicated can immediately frustrate the participant and could lead to them abandoning the survey before completing it.
- Always pilot test your online survey for any weaknesses concerning design, structure, the quality of questions being asked to participants and the length of the survey ahead of distributing it for wider data collection. This will help reduce the possibility of any under coverage and non-responses.
- On a web-based survey, sending a reminder to the sites you initially targeted that the survey remains open is likely to attract new participants who see the call for respondents for the first time.

Online survey resources

- Google Surveys – https://surveys.google.com/
- Online Surveys (UK-focused) – www.onlinesurveys.ac.uk/
- Qualtrics – www.qualtrics.com
- SurveyHero – www.surveyhero.com/
- SurveyMonkey – www.surveymonkey.com/mp/uk/

References

Benfield, J.A. and Szlemko, W.J. (2006) 'Internet-based data collection: Promises and realities'. *Journal of Research Practice*, 2 (2), Article D1: 1–15.

Cleland, J. and Cashmore, E. (2018) '"Nothing will be the same again after the Stade de France attack": Reflections of association football fans on terrorism, security and surveillance'. *Journal of Sport and Social Issues*, 42 (6): 454–469.

Cleland, J., O'Gorman, J. and Webb, T. (2018) 'Respect? An investigation into the experience of referees in association football'. *International Review for the Sociology of Sport*, 53 (8): 960–974.

Knight, C.J., Dorsch, T.E., Osai, K.V., Haderlie, K.L. and Sellars, P.A. (2016) 'Influences on parental involvement in youth sport'. *Journal of Sport, Exercise and Performance Psychology*, 5 (2): 161–178.

Murray, J. (2014) 'Survey design: Using internet-based surveys for hard-to-reach populations'. *Sage Research Methods Cases*. Available at: https://methods.sagepub.com/case/survey-design-using-internet-based-surveys-for-hard-to-reach-populations

Sue, V.M. and Ritter, L.A. (2012a) 'Sampling'. In Sue, V.M. and Ritter, L.A. (Eds.) *Conducting Online Surveys*. Thousand Oaks, CA: Sage Publications, pp. 1–12.

Sue, V.M. and Ritter, L.A. (2012b) 'Developing the survey instrument'. In Sue, V.M. and Ritter, L.A. (2012) *Conducting Online Surveys*. Thousand Oaks, CA: Sage Publications, pp. 1–31.

Vicente, P. and Reis, E. (2011) 'Internet surveys: Opportunities and challenges'. In Cruz-Cunha, M.M. and Moreira, F. (Eds.) *Handbook of Research on Mobility and Computing: Evolving Technologies and Ubiquitous Impacts*. Hershey, PA: IGI Global, pp. 805–820.

5

ONLINE INTERVIEWS

This chapter explores issues and controversies associated with interviews that are conducted online. It explains what interviews are and why they are valuable for the advancement of knowledge within the broad discipline of sport studies (as discussed in Chapter 1). It considers why and when students and researchers might choose to use online interviews as opposed to interacting with participants face-to-face, and it reflects on the benefits and limitations associated with online interviewing. Furthermore, this chapter provides practical advice for students as well as researchers who may wish to conduct online interviews in their own research projects.

KEY POINTS OF THE CHAPTER

- Understand the value of online interviews.
- Explore types of interviews.
- Recognise the advantages and disadvantages of asynchronous and synchronous online interviews.
- Prepare for conducting online interviews.
- Consider etiquette when arranging online interviews.
- Share practical tips for conducting online interviews.

Why interviews are important in sport studies

It is worth noting that interviews are the most widely used method for collecting qualitative data in sport studies. There is good reason for this too. When we know very little about a specific **phenomenon** (meaning an occurrence that is observed to happen), it makes sense to ask people who have experienced the phenomenon at first-hand about it. Speaking with members of a targeted sample is perhaps the most rudimentary and yet effective method that researchers can use to help understand any given phenomena. Interviews yield rich insights into people's experiences, aspirations, attitudes, and feelings. They can empower participants in a way that is conducive to the generation of in-depth qualitative data that would be difficult to achieve via any other means. Moreover, various interview types can be used by researchers to suit specific research objectives. We explore some of those interview types below.

Types of interviews

Structured

Imagine the following scenario. You have just received a pair of branded football boots, having ordered them via a mainstream online retailer. Two days pass and you notice an email alert from the retailer stating, 'Please share your views on the brand', or words to this effect. They incentivise you by promising to enter you into a free prize draw to win a holiday of a lifetime if you share your views. All things considered, you agree and click on the hyperlink which directs you to the research page. On the research page, the retailer emphasises the ease of the set task and the preamble explains, 'This brief interview should take no longer than three minutes to complete'. It continues, 'In addition to requesting brief demographic details (age, sex, employment status, etc.) you will be asked four main questions that are designed to gauge your views on a particular sport footwear brand'. 'Is that OK?' This all sounds fine to you (besides which, you quite fancy a holiday), so you click 'OK' and the following questions are presented:

Q1: 'What is the first thing you think of when you see this symbol?' (The symbol associated with the brand appears on your screen)

A: 'Quality is the first thing that springs to my mind. It is a symbol that I have utmost faith in. It is fashionable, all of my friends wear the brand and so do I. It is expensive though, but you get what you pay for. This brand screams quality. You pay for quality'.

Q2: 'Would you buy this brand for anyone you know?' Yes or No

A: 'Yes'.

Q3: 'If yes, who would you buy it for? (Brother/ Sister/ Mother/ Father/ Boyfriend/ Girlfriend/ Friend?)'

A: 'Brother/Sister/Boyfriend/Friend'.

Q4: 'What is it that they would like about the gift?'

A: 'It is fashionable, cool, contemporary. That is why it would not be suitable for my parents'.

You get the point – the idea of the structured interview is simple. The interviewer asks questions in a standard order and format to all participants to ensure that questions are framed in the same way and that all participants receive an identical experience. As in the example above, structured interviews can hold both quantitative and qualitative properties. Quantification is possible when answers to structured interview questions are closed ('yes' or 'no') or pre-set (such as Q3 in the example we provide above). Much like an online quantitative survey, which may list options from which the participant can choose (see Chapter 4), structured interviews can offer a similar experience. The structured interview enables researchers to add power to the findings by quoting statistical significance from a large aggregate of participants.

What structured interviews lack in depth of answers, they make up for in standardisation, reliability, credibility of research data, and time convenience (for both the researcher and the participant). As a rule of thumb, the more the researcher wishes to gain comparable data across people and across sites, the more standardised and therefore quantitative an interview tends to become. In contrast, the more the researcher wants to gather in-depth information about how individuals or groups see the world, the more he or she veers towards qualitative unstructured interviewing.

Semi-structured

Semi-structured interviews are set midway on the continuum between structured and non-structured interviews. In sport studies they are the most widely used and this is linked to the expectation that the interviewed subject's viewpoints are more likely to be expressed in an openly designed interview situation than in a standardised interview or survey questionnaire. The interview content is neither heavily restrictive nor unplanned, as the interviewer often creates a list of themes to be explored. This list, often referred to as an interview guide, is based on the evidence that exists in relation to the research topic and the studied population. The overarching idea is to use the guide to prompt the interviewee into discussion by introducing topics that the researcher would like to know more about. Those topics and questions may be addressed at some point during the interview, but the interview guide does not constrain the researcher who is free to ask additional questions based on the responses given by the participant. This allows new ideas to emerge during the interview process, helping to provide new insight into issues from the perspective of the participant.

Unstructured

Unstructured interviews are largely participant-led. This means that questions are not pre-arranged in any way and consequently, the researcher and the participant are more like equals in the research process. The researcher is merely a facilitator to the discussion. This situation allows the participant to express themselves and explain their views on their own terms, without constraint. The procedure should follow the style of an informal conversation and requires skill from the researcher to maintain a relaxed conversational style. When performed as described here, unstructured interviews are highly correlated with good rapport.

The three styles of interview outlined above form a conceptual continuum. However, it is worth noting that scholars may choose to conduct an interview that contains question types associated with all three styles. Remember, guides are there to help frame your thinking. They are not in place to stifle creativity or to hinder bespoke research models that are most appropriate for your research project. All options should remain open to ensure that the research design is applicable to the research aim(s) and objectives.

Individual activity

In what type of scenarios would it be better to use structured, semi-structured, and unstructured interviews in online research? Discuss your thoughts with a colleague.

Types of online interview

Online interviews can be defined as any dialogue or observation carried out with the aid of digital technology for the purpose of data collection (Salmons, 2015). As such they can be written or verbal and can involve carefully planned or casual interchange (including text message or social media exchange) provided that it is carried out by adhering to ethical research guidelines (see Chapter 3). The online interview is an emergent method and as such, a widely accepted set of design specifications or criteria does not exist. This should not discourage researchers from opting to use digital technology for interviewing participants. It is an exciting time to engage with online methods and to lead the way in research design.

Asynchronous online interviewing

When online interviews are not conducted 'live' or in 'real time', they are said to be **asynchronous**. The modes through which asynchronous interviews can occur are multiple and will grow into the future as new technologies or applications allow for alternative modes of communication. At present, social media communications, topic related forums, online survey technologies, **wikis**, and **blogs** are some of the routes via which researchers can engage participants in asynchronous interviews (a Wiki is a site on which multiple authors add, remove, and edit content). However, the most commonly used medium for conducting asynchronous interviews at this time is via email communication.

Asynchronous email interviews are a particularly useful form of data collection method on the basis that they allow for an extended and deliberate sequence of communications. Given that they are not conducted in real time, both researchers and participants have greater capacity to consider, reflect on, and digest messages before providing a considered response. This feature is highlighted by Kivits (2005), who explains that because participants are provided with the space to elaborate their own thinking, this allows more time for private self-focus. This aspect of asynchronous interviews is thought to be beneficial as it enables researchers to access aspects of participant lives that are normally hidden from view.

Procedure

In terms of procedure, the logistics are simple and usually follow a similar process. For example:

---

1) The researcher makes contact with potential participants, explains the research process, and gains informed consent from the participant (see Chapter 3).
2) The researcher sends a question or questions to the participant. The participant is asked to provide a considered response to them (an in-depth qualitative account) within an agreed time frame.
3) The researcher uses the response from the participant to prompt further questions, or they ask other questions that are pertinent to the research theme.
4) Once all questions have been answered, the researcher analyses the text, often using thematic, content, or framework analysis (see Chapter 7).
5) The researcher feeds back his or her findings to the participant to check for clarity and accuracy.
6) The researcher begins to write-up the project ahead of disseminating the findings once this is complete.

When highlighted in this way the procedure appears simple, though as Fritz and Vandermause (2018) explain, researchers tend to make recurring mistakes when implementing asynchronous email interviews. As such they offer practical advice that covers five main areas:

---

1) Researchers should create an email folder for each participant that takes part in their study.
2) Whilst it is possible to conduct concurrent interviews (where there is more than one interview being carried out simultaneously), this should be limited to 2–3. Without distinctive physical features (a voice or a face) to

remind the researcher who they are conversing with, there is a strong possibility that the researcher may mix up the participants when responding to more than one participant in a relatively close period of time.

3)   Interviews should be conducted in a quiet, private place that will enable the researcher to read participant responses carefully and mentally engage with them.

4)   To improve **rapport** and construct a relationship with participants, researchers have found that mimicking the participants language can be effective. When interviewing in writing, the use of **emoticons** such as the smiling face :), the open mouth smile :D, the wink ;) and the brow furrow /:, and ttyl (talk to you later) can improve the authenticity of a voice.

5)   The timings between questions ought to be carefully considered. If participants are waiting too long in between questions they might disengage from the study. Alternatively, if the timings are perceived to be too rapid, this may also discourage participation.

Tip: Fritz and Vandermause recommend that researchers should send a holding email to acknowledge receipt and to provide an indication of when they will follow up with the next response. For example, 'I received your email. Thanks so much for sharing your thoughts. I will reply and send more questions in a couple of days'.

These general recommendations are useful and ought to be carefully considered when researchers are planning to use asynchronous online interviews. However, it is equally important that researchers should remain flexible in order that they may, when suitable, provide bespoke procedures that are designed specifically for their participants. O'Connor et al. (2011) agree that flexibility relating to the detail of research design is crucial by reminding researchers that they have the freedom to decide on the best way to introduce the interview and how best to carry out the process, including how to deliver the interview questions. They insist that the interviewer can use elements of structured, semi-structured, and unstructured interview questions, to suit the requirements of the unique situation as it relates to their participants. In other words, whilst the researcher should bear in mind general rules or principles for conducting asynchronous interviews, the intricate details of the method should be figured-out with the specific experiences and requirements of the sample in mind. To provide context, perhaps a real example would be useful.

Research in sport

'The race for the café: A Bourdieusian analysis of racing cyclists in the training setting', by Rees (2016).

What was the aim of the research?

The aim was to find out what impact, if any, digital communications technology and online spaces were having on 'traditional' racing cyclist cultures.

What were the methods used?

Use of social media

Rees created a Facebook site entitled *Researching the Sociology of Cycling* and all members of the elite cyclist community were invited to join. The Facebook site offered three main advantages: (1) It would provide a focal point for the research; (2) It would allow Rees to communicate to participants on the progress of the research study; and (3) Transformative technologies would become a tool of enquiry as well as the topic. The use of Facebook as a tool of enquiry was an illustration of Rees's **reflexive** approach to the research process. To give a sense of privacy, formality, and importance to the interviews, Rees decided to collect data via email correspondence.

Obtaining informed consent online

The first step in the email interview process was for Rees to make initial contact with potential participants through a personal Facebook message to racing cyclists from the group who had 'liked' the *Researching the Sociology of Cycling* Facebook page. In this message, Rees provided study participants with information including; an outline of the research, contact details for the researcher's supervisory team (he was studying for his PhD at the time), a guarantee of anonymity and an assurance that, if agents choose to participate, their participation could cease at any time. The 'likers' were asked to provide Rees with their email address if they were willing to take part in the research. The provision of the participants' email address to Rees acted in the same way as would a signature on a paper consent form, or the clicking of a 'yes I accept' button and provided Rees with informed consent.

Strategy for collecting data

The email interviews were conducted in stages with nine questions asked (broken down into sets of three). All questions were asked in the same order on each occasion. Following a consultation with a sub-group of racing cyclists who acted as members of a **steering group** for the project (a steering group consists of experts and experts-by-experience who provide advice and aid troubleshooting on a project), a decision was taken at the outset to ensure that interview procedure was highly structured and did not allow for follow-up questions (retrospectively, this was acknowledged as a weakness of the research design). The participants were aware that they would have nine questions to answer over a period of three months. 149 email interviews were conducted between May 2014 and September 2014.

What are the advantages associated with online asynchronous interviews?

The online asynchronous interview approach has a number of distinct advantages over other forms of interviewing. The most commonly cited advantages include:

Accessibility: By using this method, the researcher can access study participants who may not be accessible in any other way. Consequently, online asynchronous interviews can increase the options that researchers have for participant recruitment.

Inclusivity: Online asynchronous interviews are perhaps the most inclusive type of interview. The flexible manner in which online asynchronous interviews are conducted ensures that most people who have a device with access to the internet can take part in any research. Ison (2009) notes how online interviews carried out asynchronously are particularly useful for those participants with verbal communication impairments. In addition, with the aid of an online translation tool, the email interview has the advantage of potentially conducting interviews in a foreign language, even if the interviewer is insufficiently fluent for a face-to-face interaction.

Considered Responses: The online asynchronous approach also allows participants to consider their responses carefully and avoid quick replies that are unlikely to provide the deep insights that the researcher requires. Consequently, online asynchronous interviews are very useful for the reflective process, which helps to assure rigour.

Flexibility for Participants: The fact that participants are free to choose when, where, and how they will answer questions can be liberating for the participant. They can answer questions at a time and location of their choosing, using any compatible digital device available to them.

Reduced Time and Financial Costs for Researchers: The response format is written and therefore the transcription is generated automatically. Consequently, the cost associated with online asynchronous interviews is low.

What are the limitations associated with online asynchronous interviews?

For all of the distinct advantages listed above, there are limitations that are specifically associated with online asynchronous interviews. Some of the most frequently cited limitations include:

Attrition Rates: Attrition for online asynchronous interviews are particularly high. The lack of social cues associated with text only interviews is often blamed for participant disengagement.

Increased Time Investment for Participants: Online asynchronous interviews increase the time investment required from participants. Interviews are often extended over weeks or months and participants can become fatigued with the process.

In summary, online asynchronous interviews are useful when the written literacy skills of the participant are strong enough to embed text-based conversations. Moreover, participants must be familiar with the platform that will be used for data collection e.g. chatroom users, bloggers, email users. Whilst this might give the impression that only the technologically skillful can participate, it is worth noting that the facilities that participants must be competent in using are considered to require low technical ability. Moreover, there are no time constraints when conducting asynchronous interviews. The participants (perhaps existing in different time zones and geographical locations) can answer questions at a time of his or her choosing, allowing for time to reflect and provide considered responses. This is a major strength as it enables participants to draft and redraft an answer, making certain that they have said exactly what they wanted to say.

Group activity

Asynchronous online interviews are often described as 'flexible' research tools. Can you provide three examples to support this assertion?

Synchronous online interviewing

An interview is **synchronous** if it is conducted in real time. It can occur via text or via audio and visual display by using a range of instant messaging or internet telephone services. But whilst it is commonly accepted that online interviewing is part of the new methodological frontier, physical co-present interviewing (otherwise known as face-to-face [FtF]) has remained the accepted practice. Face-to-face interviews are thought to provide the best opportunity for researchers to generate rich information and to create rapport by drawing on and interpreting bodily cues of the participant. However, new freely available Voice over Internet Protocol **(VoIP)** mediated technologies (such as Skype or FaceTime) are beginning to challenge this longstanding assumption.

Text-based synchronous or near-synchronous online interviews

Text-based synchronous or near-synchronous online interviews are often implemented using available internet-messaging services, which usually take the following format: (1) A conversation window is displayed for both users (the researcher and the participant); (2) The researcher types the first question, making it visible to the participant by hitting 'send'; (3) The participant responds, making his or her response visible to the researcher in the same way; (4) Dialogue is transferred between the parties using this simple system, which has benefits as well as limitations:

Benefits

Transcending geographical barriers: Like asynchronous email interviews, text-based online synchronous interviews transcend barriers of geographical distance, time, and cost associated with travelling and transcription.

Limitations

Technical competence levels: Can exclude potential participants.

Suspected multi-tasking (a feature of practice in our **multi-modal communities**): May also limit the attention that the participant is paying to the interview and hence, it may possibly affect the quality of the data.

Duration: The average duration is significantly extended for text interviews when compared to **FtF.** For example, interviews that are scheduled for one hour in the FtF mode will take approximately three hours to complete. Notwithstanding this, the word count for participant answers is reduced by half.

More physically demanding: Researchers argue that taking part in an online text-based interview is more physically demanding than a traditional interview. Participants are required to type, look at a screen, read, and make sense of questions throughout the duration of an interview. This can be fatiguing for them.

Lacking sound and vision: The lack of audio and visual aspects (traditionally associated with the FtF interview) are thought to limit the sense of emotional expression. Such circumstances are associated with ambiguity and misunderstanding when analysing the data.

Synchronous online video interviews

Some of the limitations highlighted above can be fully or partially alleviated by engaging with VoIP mediated technologies, such as Skype or FaceTime. Researchers using this technology can allow for synchronous communication including sound and video, with the option to use written text if required. Having the capacity to record audio and video at the same time without the need for additional equipment is a particular strength of Skype, which allows for quality two-way audio and/or video in free internet calls. Furthermore, it provides visual options to view a close-up picture of the participant in the room, or a wide shot of the room if there are multiple participants.

Why consider using VoIP technologies?

There are many advantages of using VoIP when interviewing. Much like other online methods, VoIP technologies transcend time and space boundaries and, when required, extend the geographical reach for any sample by connecting live with desired participants, wherever they may reside in the world (technology permitting).

Cole (2018) argues that online interviews, which use VoIP technologies, have greater flexibility than even FtF methods. Cole, and other authors too (see Hanna, 2012) argue that VoIP applications (like Skype and FaceTime) further advance the internet as a medium to create the most feasible alternative to face-to-face interviews. After all, VoIP technology enables and incorporates all of the features of a "traditional" FtF interview. The only difference being that the participants and the researcher do not need to be situated in the same location. This begs the question, how does removal of the physical space effect the rapport that is generated between the participant and the researcher in qualitative research?

Research in action

'Using video calls in qualitative (longitudinal) interviews: Some implications for rapport', by Weller (2017).

What was the aim of the research?

The aim of this research was to evaluate the nature of rapport when using online video calls.

What were the methods used?

Weller conducted 12 Skype-to-Skype and 12 Face-Time-to-Face-Time interviews with participants who were part of a longitudinal study that had previously used 'traditional' face-to-face interview techniques. This unique position allowed the participants to reflect on their experiences of partaking in both modes of interviews (FTF and online) in order to compare the experiences.

The project adopted two approaches to assess the implications of introducing internet video calls. First, it explored participant views of the shift from physical co-present to remote interviewing on relational matters (e.g. rapport, willingness to divulge). Secondly, it set out to investigate practical issues relating to the usability of new technologies (e.g. the quality of online connection, ease of use of technology). This approach sought to provide an alternative to common comparisons that tend to rely on researchers' judgements of the successes and drawbacks of VoIP interview interaction in terms of data quality.

Feedback was gathered from all participants at the end of the interview. Additionally, participants were provided with a **hyperlink** to an online survey to enable them the opportunity to leave candid response anonymously without interaction with Weller.

What were the key findings?

The findings revealed that 83 percent of participants regarded the Skype or FaceTime interview 'as good as a home visit' and all participants described feeling comfortable with a remote interview. Whilst the 'greetings' and 'leavings' (terms used by Weller to describe procedures for beginning and concluding interviews, respectively) were notably different between Skype and face-to-face interviews (Skype interviewers focusing on technicalities rather than building small talk), the rapport between Weller and participants was seemingly unaffected. In fact, less confident participants noted that they preferred to speak with researchers online. Participants explained that anxiety associated with interviews decreased as they did not have to share physical space with the researcher. With this, Weller challenges the dogma surrounding the use of synchronous online interviews.

VoIP interviews hold many advantages. They are low cost, ecological (no need to travel to a specific destination), and safe (no physical engagement). The live video feed helps to retain the personal connection without negative implications for rapport, and the interview can be downloaded immediately onto the researcher's workstation using appropriate software (with both parties captured in the recording). In short, technologies such as Skype and FaceTime retain the benefits of and (in various ways) improve on telephone and face-to-face interviews. However, before we enthrone the video interview as the new gold standard, it is important to note that technical challenges can ensue.

Challenges for VoIP interviews and troubleshooting

Multiple challenges face researchers who choose to use VoIP technologies for the purposes of research. Most notably, it is possible that a poor internet connection can drop a call, interrupt the sound quality, or pause the visual display. In such circumstances, this will affect the rapport between the participant and researcher. However, there are ways to combat such problems. For example, Seitz (2016) recommends that:

- The researcher must habitually test out the strength of online connection ahead of recording the interview.
- Both parties should have the latest version of the technology. This will ensure compatibility.
- Devices (such as computers, tablets, or smartphones) are fully charged.
- The researcher and participant discuss a strategy to minimise the risk of audio problems. (e.g. do not turn away from the microphone, avoid background noise, choose a quiet room to negate noise and distraction, remain stationary rather than walking around with a hand-held device, and speaking clearly and deliberately).
- The interview should only begin when both parties are happy.

In addition to those practical issues outlined above, Seitz argues that there are some fundamental issues with the incompatibility of this technology with emotive and sensitive situations that inevitably arise when researchers and participants discuss social phenomena. She is implying that the loss of personal connection and intimacy (because of physical separation) can make it difficult to elicit detailed answers to sensitive questions. She argues that when participants become emotional, it is more effective to respond to their needs in person.

Other researchers have found no such problems. For instance, Lo Iacono, Symonds and Brown (2016) explain that synchronised online interviews may be just as effective as face-to-face methods when dealing with sensitive issues. In fact, they argue that some participants may be more comfortable to open up via Skype because they can stay in their own safe environment without imposing on each other's personal space. Indeed, Cashmore, Cleland and Dixon (2018) infer that having physical space between the researcher and the participant enables introverted people to candidly discuss personal issues. In a sense, the screen can act as a filter for stress that is often experienced when researchers and the participant share the same space.

Group activity

Conduct a synchronous online interview on a member of your class or one of your research colleagues via Skype or FaceTime as both an interviewer and an interviewee. Reflect on the experience as: (a) the interviewer; and (b) the interviewee. Provide feedback on your experience of both roles.

Preparing and conducting online interviews

Recruiting participants

When conducting research in sport studies, access to participants is the first hurdle that researchers must face. The internet has widened the available options that researchers have by enabling them to transcend 'traditional' possibilities for recruitment. After all, the internet is a colossal expanse that touches all of our lives to varying degrees. It is a general forum for all humanity, and yet, it is possible to find tightly defined and narrow interest groups at the click of a button, or to organise participants who meet the inclusion criteria of any given study to use the internet for the purpose of interviewing.

Recent studies involving recruiting participants for online interviews on eclectic samples from the world of sport include: Elizabeth Hardy's analysis of Canadian women's rugby players in 2015; Micol Pizzolati and Davide Sterchele's discussion of mixed sex sport, featuring forced migrants in Rome in 2016; and Elizabeth Taylor and colleagues' investigation into gendered harassment in the sports management classroom in 2018. Other published works include the 2018 study of male professional 'free surfers' by Clifton Westly Evers; the 2017 investigation into the lives of middle-aged skateboarders by Paul O'Connor; and interviews with surfers on the subject of artificial waves in 2018 by Michael Roberts and Jess Pointing.

Representative samples?

In those circumstances when the internet is used to find participants, it is important that the researcher has confidence that the sample is representative. On this issue, two points are worthy of consideration. First, not everyone has an internet connection, so we must not presume complete representativeness. On a global level, Mann and Stewart (2000: 31) remind us that internet access is not only a matter of economics but also of 'place in the world' in terms of sex, culture, ethnicity, and language. Notwithstanding this, with more than four billion people logging into the internet every day (that is more than half of the world's population – as we raised in Chapter 1), it is equally important not to overlook the global and cultural reach that the internet can bring to any research project. Secondly, whilst it is theoretically possible to attain a larger sample size from online research, it is not always easy to achieve. The researcher must work hard to secure it not only by working with website providers or discussion board moderators, but also by capturing the imagination of the target audience and stimulating them enough to want to take part.

Finding a voice

Social research carried out online is particularly useful for providing a voice to groups who would otherwise be very difficult to contact or to interview face-to-face. With a considered approach, hard to reach groups (e.g. closed access when the research site is dangerous or the research topic is sensitive) can become more accessible online. For example, in sport studies, research on disability is now making use of online technology to conduct interviews in order to take into account the varied needs or requirements that disabled participants may have. In 2015, Stuart Braye used Skype interviews to overcome some of the barriers that disabled people face simply to have their voices heard via academic research. Others too have used similar approaches. Andrea Bundon and Laura Hurd Clarke conducted a study in 2015 that involved 25 Skype interviews with Paralympic athletes. Its aim was to explore how athletes with disabilities use the internet to communicate. The findings of this study outlined the liberating affordances of the internet for para-athletes. A proportion of Skype interviews were also used in a 2015 study, once again conducted by Bundon and Hurd Clarke, that examined strategies for advocating meaningful inclusion within the Paralympic Movement from the perspective of athletes.

Considering netiquette

It is important to consider **netiquette** (online etiquette) when researching participants online. For instance, it might be necessary (or advisable) to seek permissions from website providers or discussion board moderators directly before conducting research (see Chapter 3 for more detail on this). This procedure was adopted by Tom Gibbons when conducting a form of asynchronous interviews (as part of participant observation of an online community) with football fans in an online football forum in 2014. The semi-public forum had in excess of 1,000 members who would log on or off throughout the course of each day. As Gibbons describes, semi-public meant that to post on this forum agents had to enroll as members, but the content of the forum was available to anyone in the public domain.

Gibbons, aware of the guidelines provided by The Association of Internet Researchers (which concede that it is sometimes acceptable to collect data online without informed consent, providing the material is not sensitive and the online environment is public – as we discuss in Chapter 3), took the following stance. Rather than seeking consent from individual members of the football forum, he put in place steps to ensure the research was conducted in an overt fashion by declaring to the online forum moderators that he was an academic researcher interested in the views of fans who interact on the site. The forum founder agreed to allow the author access to the online community in order to conduct the research. Gibbons maintained this transparent approach with the members too. When introducing himself in what would be his first post on the forum, Gibbons used the following information to establish his authenticity as a legitimate academic researcher:

> Hi, I'm an academic researching various aspects of football fandom through asking fans their views and opinions of current issues (particularly in the English Game). **Moderators – I have requested permission from (fan 3) in admin to post on this forum**. Any information you give me will be anonymous and used solely for academic conference proceedings, journal articles, books and for teaching purposes. I will never ask for or record any information that might lead to forum members being identified. I will look forward to talking with you about your views and opinions.
>
> *(Gibbons, 2014: 167)*

Gibbons embedded his research within the online community and engaged 93 members in conversation throughout the 2008/09 football season. This method provided the researcher with a high volume of participants to contribute to this project.

Preparing an interview guide

Whether interviews are conducted using text-based methods or digital video technology, the researcher must be as fully prepared as possible. Almost all interviews apart from those that are unstructured require an interview script or guide where the interviewer records either direct questions or loose themes that they would like the participant to speak about.

Depending on interview type it is important that interviewers construct a thoughtful interview guide prior to the interview taking place. Question types will depend on the objectives of the research, but according to Kvale (2006), two types of question are often used. First, thematic questions that relate to the 'what' and 'why' of the interview; and, second, dynamic questions that expose the 'how'. In addition to the interview guide, researchers must also consider the potential probes that will be used to tactically engage the participant in further conversation, when they are required.

Individual activity

Working individually, create an interview guide on a sport-related topic of your choice. Relay your guide to a classmate or research colleague and explain your reasons for setting out your interview guide in this way. Work together to think of ways to improve the guide.

Preparing probes

The interviewer should be ready with probes that will keep the conversation going and encourage the participant to divulge information in intricate detail. According to Rubin and Rubin (2012), there are various types of probes that researchers can draw on:

Attention probes: These let the participant know that you are paying attention (either audibly or in writing). This is designed to make the participant aware that the information they are offering is important to the study's aim(s) and objectives. Attention probes such as 'I understand', 'I see', 'that is unbelievable' are based on the position that participants are experts-by-experience, and they should be treated as such by the researcher.

Clarification probes: These provide an opportunity for the researcher to pin down exactly what the participant means in their response to questions. For example, 'when you said "x" what did you mean?'

Retrospective elaboration probes: These provide the opportunity for researchers to listen to participants at first without interrupting, and then to guide them back to a potentially important feature of the interview so that a greater depth of information can be gleaned: 'Earlier you said that "other women" scoffed at your decision to try-out for the football team. Could you tell me more about that?'

Conversation management probes: These are used when the researcher needs to keep the conversation centred on a specific topic or to delve for deeper explanations of various phenomena. For example, interviewers can request more from the participant, such as 'that is interesting, can you tell me more about that?' or 'what happened next?'

Change of direction probes: These are used in order to expand the topic into a new area. For example, 'You have told me about how you trained as a male gymnast; can you now tell me how your friends at school reacted to this news?'

Non-verbal probes: These can be used in online video technology interviews when the participant and the researcher can see one another. A nod of the head, a gaze, and a facial impression can encourage the speaker to continue with their response to a question.

Probes are crucial for making the most of any qualitative interview in order to get as much detail out of a participant as possible. Probes serve to increase the sense of rapport between the researcher and participant and improve the experience for both parties in the process. The key to success is preparation aligned with human abilities to listen, speak when it is appropriate to do so, and be able to hold a conversation.

Practice makes perfect

Every researcher becomes more skilled and competent at specific tasks with experience. This is where practice interviews (with at least one person who is not a research participant) can enable researchers to experience the interview process and iron out any issues that may emerge as a result. It is recommended that even experienced researchers should conduct practice interviews when handling new technology. The practice run will help the researcher to anticipate any technological problems and to think about contingency plans. Some useful questions to consider:

- Did the participant receive information on the purpose of the interview, their role, and estimated length of duration of the interview?
- Were the ground rules (if any) clearly explained to the participant?
- How clear are the log-in instructions for the participant?
- Do you have the telephone number of the participant in case you need to switch methods at the last minute due to technical problems?

If conducting text-based interviews, it is arguably more important that the researcher is prepared in order to hold the attention of the participant and to keep the interview running smoothly. In all eventualities the researcher should attempt to place themselves in the shoes of the participant and pre-prepare definitions of terms or clarifications of concepts related to the research phenomenon. Such detail, written out beforehand, could be cut and then pasted into the interview text as required. Researchers should also familiarise themselves with the target population use of emoticons or text speech.

To save time during the online interview, participants should be encouraged to use text speech as long as meanings associated with it are clear. Likewise, emoticons such as ☺ ☹ can be used to provide social cues as to emotion of the participant and intent of the verbatim statements. It is recommended that where emoticons are used, researchers should set out consistent meaning associated with each one. This can be posted to the participant in advance of the interview or the researcher can create an information-holding website that all participants can access. Organisational information, and shared images or files can all be uploaded to this holding-information website.

Conclusion

This chapter has focused on the value of online interviews in addressing the aim(s) and objectives of a research project. It has explained that whilst interviews are often considered to be the most basic form of empirical data collection, they provide an effective means of collating valuable data that is often rich in quality. Interviews are a 'natural' means of extracting information from other humans and this method has been practiced since time immemorial. They rely on basic procedures that draw on our ability to communicate using various modes of discourse. In our contemporary screen-laden societies, the potential to interview has now moved online.

When conducting online interviews, researchers can opt to interview via asynchronous (not in real time) or synchronous (in real time) methods. In this chapter we have discussed the advantages and disadvantages of both interview styles and have explained how to use each for maximum impact. Whilst we recognise that the online interview is an emergent method without widely accepted design specifications or criteria to draw on, we argue that researchers should not be discouraged from opting to use the internet when interviewing participants. This is an exciting time to engage with online methods and to lead the way in research design.

References

Cashmore, E., Cleland, J. and Dixon, K. (2018) *Screen Society*. London: Palgrave.

Cole, A. (2018) 'Online interviews'. In Allen, M. (Ed.) *The Sage Encyclopedia of Communication Research Methods*. Available at: https://methods.sagepub.com/reference/the-sage-encyclopedia-of-communication-research-methods

Fritz, R. and Vandermause, R. (2018) 'Data collection via in-depth email interviewing: Lessons from the field'. *Qualitative Health Research*, 28 (10): 1640–1649.

Gibbons, T. (2014) *English National Identity and Football Fan Culture: Who Are Ya?* London: Ashgate.

Hanna, P. (2012) 'Using internet technologies (such as Skype) as a research medium: A research note'. *Qualitative Research*, 12 (2): 239–242.

Ison, N. (2009) 'Having their say: E-mail interviews for research data collection with people who have verbal communication impairment'. *International Journal of Social Research Methodology*, 12 (2): 161–172.

Kivits, J. (2005) 'Online interviewing and the research relationship'. In Hine, C. (Ed.) *Virtual Methods: Issues in Social Research on the Internet*. Oxford: Berg, pp. 35–50.

Kvale, S. (2006). 'Dominance through interviews and dialogues'. *Qualitative Inquiry*, 12 (3): 480–500.

Lo Iacono, V., Symonds, P. and Brown, D. (2016) 'Skype as a tool for qualitative research interviews'. *Sociological Research Online*, 21 (2): 1–15.

Mann, C. and Stewart, F. (2000) *Internet Communication and Qualitative Research*. London: Sage Publications.

O'Connor, H., Madge, C., Shaw, R. and Wellens, J. (2011) 'Internet based interviewing'. In Fielding, N., Raymond, M. and Blank, G. (Eds.) *The Sage Handbook of Online Research Methods*. London: Sage Publications, pp. 271–289.

Rees, T. (2016) 'The race for the café: A Bourdieusian analysis of racing cyclists in the training setting'. Unpublished Ph.D. Thesis. Teesside University, UK.

Rubin, H. and Rubin, I. (2012) *Qualitative Interviewing: The Art of Hearing Data*. London: Sage Publications.

Salmons, J. (2015) *Qualitative Online Interviews* (2nd Edition). London: Sage Publications.

Seitz, S. (2016) 'Pixilated partnerships, overcoming obstacles in qualitative interviews via Skype: A research note'. *Qualitative Research*, 16 (2): 229–235.

Taylor, E., Hardin, R. and Rode, C. (2018) 'Contrapower harassment in the sport management classroom'. *NASPA Journal About Women in Higher Education*, 11 (1): 17–32.

Weller, S. (2017) 'Using video calls in qualitative (longitudinal) interviews: Some implications for rapport'. *International Journal of Social Research Methodology*, 20 (6): 613–625.

6

INVESTIGATING THE ONLINE WORLD

The purpose of this chapter is to highlight how online observation, or 'netnography', can be used to help researchers understand and make sense of online behaviour, cultures, and communities. The chapter begins by defining and discussing ethnography, before exploring netnography, as this traditional method is now being carried out online. The various forms and approaches of ethnography and netnography will be considered and the similarities and differences between them. The chapter will then explain how netnography can be used, and how the data can be captured and analysed. It also highlights the advantages and limitations of netnography and offers tips to online researchers when adopting this methodological approach.

KEY POINTS OF THE CHAPTER

- Identify the difference between ethnography and netnography.
- Recognise the different approaches and forms of netnography that are available.
- Understand the importance of immersion in an online community.
- Acknowledge the ways in which researchers can enter the online community under investigation.
- Understand field notes, the importance of them, and how to take them whilst undertaking research in an online community.
- Awareness of reflexivity and how to work reflexively in your own research.
- Identify the ethical considerations when conducting netnography.

What is ethnography?

Ethnography, put simply, means to write about the 'way of life', or culture, of social groups. Salmons (2016: 28–29) suggests that such studies focus on culture(s) and cultural influences and attempt to describe and interpret cultural behaviour by 'emphasizing the importance of understanding the meanings and cultural practices of people within everyday contexts'. Ethnographers undertake holistic research, seeking to 'understand shared practices, meanings, and social contexts, and the interrelations among them' (Boellstorff et al., 2012: 67). For Boellstorff et al. (2012: 65), 'ethnographers have an extremely broad methodological palette' and work can include a wide variety of methodological tools. However, observation is the fundamental component of ethnography. While the qualitative researcher may spend weeks or months in the field conducting face-to-face interviews, the ethnographer, on the other hand, invests considerable time gathering data with study participants, either overtly or covertly, and watches what happens, listens to what is said, and depending on the researcher's positionality, asks questions to help holistically complement the study's aim(s) and objectives.

ETHNOGRAPHIC ORIGINS

Although ethnography appears to have Greek roots (*ethnos* "people", *graphein* "writing"), the term ethnography was coined in 1767 by Johann Friedrich Schöpperlin, during the German Romanticism period (Boellstorff et al., 2012). During the nineteenth century, travellers, traders, explorers, and missionaries would document their observations without academic positions. Due to the segregated nature of 'fieldworkers' and 'theorists' at this time, it was the armchair scholars who made sense of ethnographic fieldworkers' writings. For example, influential scholars central to the early twentieth-century anthropological movement such as E.B. Taylor (1871) and James Frazer (1915) never got their 'hands dirty' in the field (Boellstorff et al., 2012). Despite ethnography being coined in the mid-to-late eighteenth century, almost 150 years passed until the modern conception of the 'ethnographic researcher' was born. Classical social anthropologist, Bronislaw Malinowski (1884–1942), is considered an ethnographic pioneer as he became the first researcher to unite 'fieldworker' and 'theorist' in a singular figure – the 'ethnographer'. Malinowski, who researched the Trobriand Islanders, near Papua New Guinea, between 1914–18, 'joined their communities, learned their language and lived among them as a member, noting and recording his observations in preparation for writing about them later' (McNeil and Chapman, 2005: 90). Unlike former works, Malinowski brought together method and theory, which is central to our understanding of ethnography.

From the 1930s onwards, the Chicago School, led by Robert E. Park, followed in the footsteps of pioneering social anthropologists Bronislaw Malinowski, D.T. Evans-Pritchard, and Margaret Mead. Park encouraged his students to 'go get the seat of your pants dirty in real research' (Pollner and Emerson, 2001: 130). The School was famous for employing ethnographic methods to help understand various social groups, with a particular focus on the poor and the deviant. The Chicago School demonstrated the importance and power of anthropological and sociological research as it helps provide a voice for groups and communities who are often ignored by the institutions that actively shape them. Although ethnographic methods disappeared somewhat during the mid-twentieth century, within British sociology at least, pupils of the Park generation such as Howard Becker and Erving Goffman re-popularised such methods during the late 1960s. The classic works of Malinowski, Mead, Park, and Goffman have undoubtedly helped shape ethnographic methods and techniques. Now, with the advent of the internet, researchers have the ability to critically investigate and observe online communities, understanding how they behave, interact, and communicate.

Although there is no 'hard or fast' rule regarding how to conduct an ethnography or observation, as we shall now discuss below, there are three principal ways or broad approaches in which to undertake ethnographic research: Direct or **non-participant observation**; **participant observation**; and **complete participant**.

Direct or non-participant observation

Popularly used within sociology between the 1960s and 1980s, particularly within classroom contexts, the researcher becomes a detached onlooker. The ethnographer usually designs a structured approach to observation whereby a quantifiable coding schedule is established. This method focuses on 'types of behaviour or activity; activity that does not fit the schedule is ignored' (McNeil and Chapman, 2005: 92). In turn, this method is useful for capturing and classifying behaviour into separate categories. For example, this approach could be taken to critically examine performances of masculinity among cricket fans during a Test Match (a form of the game lasting up to five days). The unobtrusive ethnographer could code the frequency of 'heckles' from the stand, the types of chants performed, and/or clothing choices. While pen and paper were once the only way to quantify such codes, researchers are now able to be more discreet than ever before using smart phones or tablets to capture the data.

Participant observation

Participant observation is the most common method employed. McNeil and Chapman (2005: 95) state that this approach 'involves the sociologist being on the inside because he or she joins in with the activities of those being studied and shares their experiences of social reality'. The researcher announces themselves to their informants from the beginning, usually with the aid of gatekeepers who grant and facilitate their entry into the respective online community. Data is thus generated from the 'inside' rather than the 'outside', and this method requires skill, diligence, and patience. Burdsey's fieldwork between 2000 and 2004 into British Asians and football employed participant observation techniques as he watched matches with supporters, and interacted with players, coaches, and club members before and after games and training sessions (see Burdsey, 2007). His experiences illustrate the benefits of this approach as 'these occasions provided the opportunity to watch, listen, enjoy stories, share the joys and sorrows of a game, and recognise the special exchanges and rituals intrinsic to football' (Burdsey, 2007: 6). As this study demonstrates, the 'insider' position allows the researcher to understand how groups construct identities and form notions of belonging.

Complete participant

The complete participant hides their true identity and motives from the group. The ethnographer spends a considerable amount of time within the group, full-time for several months or even years, in the hope that their presence is taken for granted and the groups' behaviour returns to 'normal'. While Giulianotti (1995) chose to become a participant observer during his investigation into football hooliganism, Armstrong (1998) preferred complete participation as he believed that the potential 'deviant' acts among the hooligans would be more prevalent without an overt researcher present. Not surprisingly, this position raises a whole host of ethical questions and dilemmas which we will discuss later in this chapter (see also Chapter 3).

In short, *non-participant observation*, *participant observation*, and *complete participant observation* all refer to the ethnographic researcher's positionality. It must be emphasised that these three ethnographic approaches also apply to online ethnography.

Group activity

Discuss whether you would select non-participant observation, participant observation, or complete participant observation for the below research questions and why:

1   Undertake a critical examination of masculinity within sports coaching qualification courses.
2   Cricket has traditionally been labelled the 'gentleman's game'. To what extent do you agree with this within contemporary cricket fandom.
3   An investigation into whether grassroots tennis clubs are economically exclusive.

Forms of ethnography

It is important to highlight and understand that various forms, or styles, of ethnography exist. Choosing which form depends on the research aim(s). Forms of ethnography include critical realist (Atkinson, 2016), institutional (Norstedt and Paulsen, 2016), auto-ethnographic (Villegas, 2018), performative (Thrift, 2007), and sensory (Pink, 2015). While these do not necessarily incorporate new media technologies, it is audience ethnography and visual ethnography in particular whereby technology and media are centred. Table 6.1 defines the various forms of ethnography available to researchers.

TABLE 6.1 Forms of Ethnography

Forms of ethnography	Description
Audience	Audience ethnography observes how people actively engage or consume specific mediated or physical-cultural texts. Participants, individually or in small groups, may watch, listen, or read a text while the ethnographer observes their live reactions to the content. This form of ethnography often includes focus group scenarios whereby the researcher facilitates discussions. Qualitative responses gathered in focus groups are useful for the researcher and this could be the only method adopted. However, choosing an audience ethnographic approach allows for deeper data as the researcher can comprehend how audiences decode content 'live'.
Auto-ethnographic	Autoethnography aims to describe and analyse personal experience to comprehend cultural phenomena. The researcher develops a question in response to a particular cultural process or experience and then reflexively describes and examines their own account of the process or experience. Within this approach, the researcher uses elements of autobiography and ethnography to write autoethnography. We look within ourselves and the community under investigation for answers.
Critical realist	Critical realist ethnography focuses on the social structures and systems that control and shape life. People are both empowered and constrained by social structures, environmental factors, and one's own personal motivations. Critical realism helps us critically understand the mechanisms that influence human action.
Institutional	Institutional ethnography investigates the social relations that work to structure people's day-to-day lives. It centralises the ways in which people interact with one another, and form relationships and understandings, within the context of social institutions (family, workplaces, media, universities, sports clubs). Otherwise called *standpoint ethnography*, it explores peoples' experiences and how they are influenced by the cultural practices of social institutions.

(Continued)

TABLE 6.1 (Continued)

Forms of ethnography	Description
Performative	This arts-based approach attempts to bridge the gap between academia and the public. After immersion within the group, the researcher will create a performance piece (theatre or screen) alongside some of the participants under study. This performance can generate impact as it attempts to educate wider audiences on the phenomenon under investigation.
Sensory	Sensory ethnography is an approach to conducting ethnography that centres our sensory perceptions, sensory experiences, and sensory categories that we use to describe events or moments in our daily lives. It operates under the belief that human meaning is not only created through language, but also through pre- or non-linguistic processes, in which sensory experience is paramount.
Visual	Visual ethnography is particularly useful for researchers who intend for their participants to tell their own stories, from their own visual vantage points. Subjects are encouraged to take photographs, videos, and drawings of people, spaces, or events that are particularly meaningful to them. This methodological approach empowers the research participants and arguably further limits the researchers' subjectivity, bias, and influence.

So far, we have defined ethnography, highlighted how it has advanced and evolved as a research tool, discussed the three broad approaches to conducting ethnographic fieldwork, and critically explored multiple forms of ethnography, some of which centre on new media technologies. The following section defines netnography and highlights the various forms of netnographic approaches available to researchers who look to the internet for this research method.

Netnography

Netnography is an ethnographic tool employed when investigating social interaction in online spaces. Primarily a qualitative method, it adapts ethnographic studies of cultures and communities in the context of computer-mediated technologies. Otherwise known as 'digital ethnography', 'virtual ethnography', 'internet ethnography', or 'cyberethnography', we prefer the neologism netnography (internet and ethnography). Instead of being embroiled in a lengthy debate about terminology, netnography, quite simply, is preferred because the internet, and thus the 'net', 'refers to a network of networks through which the data of cyberspace are transmitted' (Gaiser and Schreiner, 2009: 7). It is this network of networks that netnographers critically investigate. The term netnography encompasses virtual methods (online surveys, online interviews), digital methods (hyperlink analysis, web content analysis, social media research), and our conception of cyberspace (the storage, modification, and exchange of data). Without the 'net', none of the above would be possible, or even exist. Netnography is thus the shorthand way of encompassing the above contenders. For Salmons (2016), there are three ways in which the online researcher, or netnographer, can gather data: **Extant, elicited, enacted**.

Extant researchers

Extant researchers read, copy, or download data that is already available online. Communication via websites, blogs, or social media platforms may be observed and analysed, with the researcher remaining hidden, having no direct contact with the users. Extant research can be conducted synchronously (e.g. real-time social media posts captured during a basketball game) or asynchronously (e.g. archived social media posts examined over the course of a basketball season).

Elicited research

Elicited research relies on direct interaction with informants. As the term implies, researchers elicit a participant's responses to questions or other prompts. For example, 'researchers using participant observation online may post to a social media or online community site' (Salmons, 2016: 8). The researcher may become a part of the online community under investigation, but this raises ethical questions around the reliability of the data as the researcher may have influenced, or elicited, certain responses and thus the results (for a broader discussion on this see Chapter 3).

Enacted research

Enacted research refers to an activity or event which is constructed by the researcher that allows the data to flow. Enacted researchers generally adapt and employ traditional qualitative methods such as role-plays, simulations, or games.

It is important to point out that these three online approaches share clear similarities and overlaps with the three broad types of traditional ethnography: *Direct observation, participant observation*, and *complete participant* that we highlighted earlier in this chapter.

The rise of netnography

Bundon (2016) rightly points out that in the 'new media' era, where contemporary media forms are no longer considered 'new' and where digital technologies are manifest within our daily routines, it seems redundant to ask qualitative researchers whether they will or will not use the internet in their research project. Rather, it is a case of 'how' researchers will use the internet. Unsurprisingly, then, there has been an increase of netnographic research within sport studies in recent years.

Research in sport

- Abeza et al. (2017) critically investigated social media and relationship marketing in professional team sports. Using netnography, they examined how teams from the four major North American professional sports leagues (i.e. NBA, NFL, MLB, NHL) use social media as a relationship marketing tool. Their 'immersion into the "culture" and extensive and deep exposure to the setting' allowed them to 'gain insight into various ways that professional teams attempt to communicate and cocreate added value through interaction with their fans' (Abeza et al., 2017: 331).
- Likewise, Hambrick and Kang (2014) explored Pinterest as a relationship marketing tool also within the four major North American sports leagues, noting that Pinterest is employed to promote and develop the fan group experience, and sell team-related merchandise.
- Wallace-McRee and Lee (2016) examined the way in which the NFL facilitated loyalty and belonging via Facebook and official websites, finding that Facebook played a key role in nurturing relationships and promoting team partners.
- Numerato (2015) used netnography to investigate the use of social media by football supporters and football clubs in three European nations, alongside face-to-face (offline) observations, to understand the differences in fan behaviour between online and offline spaces.
- Cleland and Cashmore (2016); Farrington et al. (2015); Hynes and Cook (2013); and Kilvington and Price (2017, 2019), among others, have used extant techniques to capture data in relation to the discrimination, trolling, and abuse that sports stars, teams, and fans encounter on social network sites. These extant and elicited studies could have been conducted via other techniques such as interviews or surveys. However, it could be argued that richer data has been generated or constructed because netnography allows a more holistic picture to be revealed.

Immersion

Ethnographic **immersion** in the research field is essential. Researchers must 'prepare to devote substantial amounts of time in the ethnographic endeavour' (Boellstorff et al., 2012: 76). This deep immersion in the everyday life practices of communities allows us to really learn, know, and represent the participants under study. In his use of ethnographic methods to examine boxing subcultures, Sugden (1996: 201) argues that:

> It is only through total immersion that he or she can become sufficiently conversant with the formal and informal rules governing the webbing of the human interaction under investigation so that its innermost secrets can be revealed.

Not only does greater time in the field allow for an increased understanding of cultures, processes, and behaviours, but simply 'being there' is important as we do not know when interesting and noteworthy events will occur. Ethnography, and netnography, thus relies on accessing the 'lived experiences' of the communities under investigation. It is about imitating 'real' life. It is about being able to 'empathise with or think like the people that are being studied' (McNeil and Chapman, 2005: 90). And, it is about becoming part of the community under investigation, depending on the researchers' positionality.

Enter the common question: 'How long should an ethnographer spend in the field?' Well, ethnographers walk, they do not run, let alone sprint. Ethnography is often a marathon, not a sprint. Traditionally, ethnographers would spend one year, perhaps more, in the field. However, in contemporary research the amount of time can differ. For example, 'If we have conducted preliminary fieldwork, or do not need to learn a new language', unlike Malinowski in his investigation of the Trobriand Islanders, 'the time necessary for participant observation may be considerably less than a year' (Boellstorff et al., 2012: 88–89). Nonetheless, the general rule for those undertaking a netnography, certainly those favouring a participant observation or elicited approach, would be to spend 'several hours [per day] inworld for purposes of immersion' (Boellstorff et al., 2012: 89).

To summarise, there is no definitive answer regarding how long you spend in the field as it is completely project dependent. While some ethnographic projects last weeks or months, others can last years. Projects which employ netnographic methods over a shorter length of time usually adopt the phrase of observation instead or note that they utilise elements of netnography. This data is often presented in pilot studies and built upon in longer-term research projects where immersion can be fully achieved. Undergraduate researchers, who usually embark upon shorter-term research projects, often use convenience sampling for netnography whereby some form of understanding and relationship is already established as this can save a significant amount of time (see Chapter 2). If you are interested in using netnography within your sport studies project, ask yourself:

- Are you an existing member of a sporting fan forum?
- Do you already follow or converse with sporting fan groups on social media platforms?
- If you play for a sports team, do you have a social media group chat?
- Do you belong to a fantasy sports league?
- Are you part of an online sports gaming community?

Any of these topics can be critically investigated. If you are already a member, for instance, immersion is a real possibility. For members, access can be relatively straight forward, but we must consider the various ways in which researchers can enter the online community.

Entering the online community

Kozinets (2006) states that there are four procedures when studying online communities using a netnographic approach:

(1) Entering the community.
(2) Collecting and analysing the data.
(3) Conducting ethical research.
(4) Providing the participants with the opportunity to feedback to the researcher.

This chapter explores all four procedures, but it is the first procedure, making a cultural entrée, that this section will now critically examine. There are two categories related to the reason or motivation for entrée. On the one hand, *opportunistic* researchers are those who 'may be born into a group, thrown into a group by chance circumstance (e.g. illness), or have acquired intimate familiarity through occupational, recreational, or lifestyle participation' (Anderson, 2006: 379). On the other hand, the researcher might become a *convert*, meaning that they 'enter the community after starting a study and become immersed in its culture' (Villegas, 2018: 248). It is likely that undergraduate netnographers will be opportunistic rather than converts.

Researchers make key decisions about *how* they intend to enter the online research environment and what their presence will be. Bundon (2016: 360–361) summarises the four positions available:

> Lurking (observing and collecting data while remaining invisible to those they are researching); partial disclosure (for example, contacting site administrators or forum moderators, asking for consent to study the group); full disclosure (introducing themselves to online participants and/or seeking consent from each individual); and finally, participatory methods (disclosing their presence and actively engaging with participants in a collaborative fashion).

'Lurkers' consume online content, such as reading Tweets or Facebook posts, but do not themselves contribute to any online discussion. While in the face-to-face world this position would be difficult to adopt, the internet has provided a space where researchers can stay completely invisible and collect data in a natural setting. Conversely, researchers who choose to announce themselves, and thus be overt, must decide which approach is best suited to meet the study's aim(s) and objectives. Boellstorff et al. (2012: 77) argue that researchers begin by reaching out and 'should be upfront from the outset, explaining in clear language the goals of the research, what we want to do and for how long'. They continue, stating that gatekeepers or key informants play a vital role in the research process. Gatekeepers unlock doors, or open the gates, and allow us into the community under investigation. Do not underestimate the importance of these figures 'as they can often enhance and deepen the ethnographer's knowledge of the culture, serve as researcher advocates and provide entrée to other informants within the community' (Boellstorff et al., 2012: 79). It must be noted, however, that gatekeepers should not be the sole point of our observations and, as McNeil and Chapman (2005: 107) indicate, institutional gatekeepers, in particular, 'may have an agenda of their own, and they may wish to control how you observe and what you observe'. As researchers, then, we must always remain critical when investigating communities, and this certainly extends to gatekeepers.

Boellstorff et al. (2012: 76) state that 'preparing the research self is establishing the type of presence we wish to have within the worlds we are studying'. The researcher must therefore decide whether they want to be an 'outsider' (i.e. lurker) conducting extant research or an 'insider' (i.e. full disclosure) collecting elicited or enacted data.

Outsider (also labelled etic) researchers rely on secondary sources to help shape and identify their research questions while **insider** (also labelled emic) researchers 'draw on their own knowledge of issues and problems to identify research questions' (Salmons, 2016: 100). VanDeVen (2007) contrasts these two positions suggesting that outsider researchers remain detached, impartial onlookers while insider researchers are immersed within the communities being investigated. Although it appears that researchers must make a conscious choice between being an insider or outsider, ethnographic approaches commonly draw on both insider and outsider forms of analysis. These forms of analyses overlap as the researcher may fluctuate between insider and outsider perspectives at different stages of the investigation. As Salmons (2016: 102) notes, 'the insider may begin with questions that emerged from experience, then generate new areas of inquiry after consulting the literature'. Flawed or incomplete ethnographic studies often confuse which claims and conclusions derive from outsider (from the perspective of the observer) or insider (from the perspective of the participant) viewpoints. This highlights the importance of clarity and transparency within the processes of data collection.

To end on a cautionary note, we must enter the research field with focus or at least, a set of research aims and objectives that can help centre, position, or guide our observations. As Holt and Sparkes (2001: 242) rightly state, upon entering the community, the ethnographer must 'suspend a wide range of common-sense and theoretical knowledge in order to minimise the danger of taking on misleading preconceptions about the setting and the people in it'. Opportunistic researchers have the difficulty of making the familiar seem strange while convert researchers learn to view the strange with familiarity. Nevertheless, whatever approach the researcher adopts, whether it is an 'insider' or 'outsider' position, maintaining analytical distance is essential. Kozinets (2006) suggests that the second stage of online research is collecting and analysing the data. This is where we now turn our attention.

Using netnography

The central component of netnography is observation. Yet, observation is often complimented alongside other methods.

EXAMPLE

A football manager is the nucleus of the football team but he or she is supported by fellow coaches, scouting analysts, physio's, etc. These figures work together and contribute towards the output or goal, i.e. the team's results. The manager needs help, assistance, and support to achieve the best results. When AFC Bournemouth's manager Eddie Howe won the English Premier League Manager of the Month award in October 2018, he posed with the award alongside his fellow staff to showcase that the manager is part of a wider team. Like the football manager, observation within netnography is also the core of the research. But, observation often relies on additional support and methods to help probe, shape, and clarify emerging themes and ideas. Put simply, these additional methods help unlock different types of data and thus potentially improve the output, i.e. the results of the research. While a manager can utilise their assistants and fellow coaches, ethnographers can employ interviews and surveys, to achieve better results.

Observation captures unique and essential data, but results can be limited unless additional methodological approaches are incorporated. Hine (2012) notes that qualitative and quantitative methods are common-place and complimentary within online research as it helps us understand the big picture. As context is very hard for the online researcher to understand, online interviews and online surveys help us holistically make sense of the data. These methods therefore clarify things we cannot see such as whether the participant agonised or deliberated over a word choice within a social media post or whether a reply was sent with consideration or haste. McNeil and Chapman (2005: 114) add that 'interviews are sometimes useful as a tool of validation in that the observer can ask members of the group how they saw certain events to ensure that the researcher's field notes contain an authentic picture of what went on'. This, for example, helps the researcher clarify their insider and outsider positionality. Put simply, 'the combination of data can act as a resource to generate a more complex understanding of people's lives' (Smith, 2013: 111).

Field notes

Field notes are an essential component of netnographic study. These are the observational writings (notes) the researcher captures while spending time within the research environment (field). Auto-netnographers take reflexive field notes which become a record of their own observations relating to their emotions and experiences of their time online. When we are lurking, or participating within group discussions, we must remain critical and take note of what we observe, hear, see, sense, feel, and experience. Arguably, capturing field notes is much easier online than in the face-to-face world as online researchers have the benefit of screen-recording, taking screenshots, and 'two-boxing' (controlling two computers concurrently with one for immersion and the other for taking field notes). Netnographers may decide to take 'scratch-notes' (small notes) during the session which allows them to devote greater attention to the research participants. Boellstorff et al. (2012) posit that researchers taking 'scratch-notes' should expand or refine these within a 24-hour window. They also add that online researchers should 'err on the side of over-notating' when conducting the fieldwork because if we do not write it down, it might as well never have happened (Boellstorff et al., 2012: 82). Researchers should record as much data as possible and as your investigations develop, you become more selective and refined in what you record.

The observation process and reflexivity

Thorpe and Olive (2016: 130) note the three stages of the observation process:

> Descriptive observations – during which the researcher aims to record all possible details; focused observation – refers to more specific observation that concentrates on more defined activity or location in the field; and selective observations – refers to further specified observation of a more specific aspect of an activity or location.

Throughout this process, the ethnographer must remain critical and reflexive. '**Reflexivity** is a researcher's critical self-awareness of personal values, beliefs, and preferences, where these have originated from, and why' (Schinke and Blodgett, 2016: 88). Gratton and Jones (2014) add that reflexive ethnographers assess their own position, critically analysing the power relations between themselves and the participants in their search for 'truth'. Netnographers should present transparent work which showcases 'stories from the field'. These stories should account for the social processes, and especially the actions of the researcher, and how these actions impinge upon and contribute to the 'construction' of knowledge.

Analysing the data

When researchers analyse data, it is not the end, it is not the beginning, but it is part of a continual process. When netnographers enter the field, observations will commence, questions may be asked, and field notes will be captured. The research will become more focused and refined the more time the researcher spends in the field. Themes and patterns shift into focus and some research avenues appear more interesting and noteworthy than others. Probing further into emerging themes and going deeper is all connected with data analysis as netnographers should be constantly writing up their field notes and making sense of them to further guide the study. Analysing, or **coding**, the data is thus like a conveyor belt, it is constantly moving forward, it is always in process. We must not envisage data analysis as the final point of the study, then, but train ourselves to analyse and reflect on the data consistently from the study's beginning to end (see Chapter 7).

Organising the data is therefore an important part of the research and if organised well, it can save the researcher a significant amount of time. Hand-written field notes are arguably rather archaic now and we suggest using a word-processer to electronically capture and store the documents. As a result, when themes emerge you can store these records under the relevant file name and keep adding documents. For example, a study which aims to investigate fan discussions in the build up to Ultimate Fighting Championship (UFC) matches might generate themes of 'aggression', 'trash-talk', or 'tactics' after observing online debates. Any comment that relates to these themes would be captured and saved within the relevant file. The more time the researcher spends in the field observing, the larger the file becomes as more data is gathered and saved. For Adler and Adler (1994: 381), a 'funnel' approach to observation is advised as researchers should progressively narrow their attention into deeper elements of the setting. On some occasions, initial themes might become split into sub-categories or sub-themes. For Hine (2012), this is simply part of the research process as ethnographers should aim to edit down the conversations and observations in order to fully understand and make sense of them.

Finally, it is important to consider objectivity and subjectivity in the observational and data analysis process. Rather than envisaging some sort of 'pure' or objective observation, the consensus is that researchers can and do influence the results in some way. Put simply, the researcher is a fundamental component in the research – their culture and past experiences, and their sex, age, ethnicity, religion, gender, sexual orientation, class, etc. may all affect how they interpret their data and findings, but also, these social demarcations shape the interactions, relationships, and observations they are able to access. Thorpe and Olive (2016: 133) offer sound advice as 'the key is to critically reflect upon how the researcher's subjectivities inform all stages of the research process, including the gathering of "data" from the field'. Rather than deny that researchers influence the data, we should instead acknowledge interpretivist paradigms and reflect on how our identities impact on the results. This reflexivity can thus become part of the data analysis and the researcher's overall research findings.

Netnography: Why do we study online communities?

According to Hine (2012), high quality online research tells us something significant about how the contemporary world is organised and experienced. Of course, our webs of social relationships, whether it is personal or professional, extend to cyberspace. As Hine (2012) notes, the internet is a space in which meaningful interactions take place. Gaiser and Schreiner (2009: 5) add that, 'any place where people interact online represents a potential place where interactants can be observed and discussions can be analysed'. As researchers, we critically investigate online meanings to comprehend and conceptually illuminate how culture is created and developed. For Boellstorff et al. (2012: 1), virtual worlds are worthy of investigation as they are 'valid venues for cultural practice, seeking to understand both how they resemble and how they differ from other forms of culture'. They continue, suggesting that netnography and immersion is the preferred methodological tool to fully critically comprehend online cultures and communities. As researchers, we must critically scrutinise the online methods available to us and highlight the advantages and disadvantages of netnography.

ADVANTAGES OF NETNOGRAPHY

- It is more convenient, cheaper, and accessible than traditional (face-to-face) ethnography.
- It is easier to study 'hard to reach' populations using netnography.
- It is perhaps easier to study more sensitive subjects.
- It is easier to capture and log the data, e.g. two-boxing, screenshots, instant digital field notes, etc.
- Visual anonymity can provide a higher degree of safety for the researcher, especially if deviant groups are being investigated.
- Extant researchers have the ability to examine years of archived social media posts thus understanding the online community without having to invest years of time within the data collection stage. In short, netnographic archival studies can save the researcher a significant amount of time.

DISADVANTAGES OF NETNOGRAPHY

- The researcher may face a lack of confidence regarding their IT and digital skills. Some researchers may thus be at a disadvantage as 'conducting research in virtual worlds requires acquiring considerable expertise, not only in the culture being studied but in the mechanics of the software itself' (Boellstorff et al., 2012: 74).
- The researcher is unable to fully ensure truthfulness and engagement when conducting observations or online interviews with online participants. Video interviews or web-cams could help overcome such limitations.
- Researchers may misunderstand or misinterpret their observations. To overcome this limitation, researchers could employ online interviews or online focus groups to understand the phenomenon correctly.

- It has been suggested that insider online researchers struggle to be objective because they are researching the community that they are from. Yet, as noted earlier, this can often benefit or strengthen the study. For Boellstorff et al. (2012: 41), 'subjectivity is an inescapable condition' of the research process as 'no pure realm of objectivity exists'.
- In addition, the researcher's presence (elicited or enacted) might affect the environment. That said, 'the ethnographer can add new perspectives but does not shatter a fragile unity. Were cultures so vulnerable to change, they would not persist over time or in the face of disagreement, debate, external influence, and displacement' (Boellstorff et al., 2012: 45). This argument indicates that the researcher does not significantly impact on the group's behaviour. We would add that researchers who immerse themselves within the field and become an accepted member of the community arguably have a decreased impact on the results compared to those who spend less time within the community. The skills of the researcher are important here as rapport must be created and developed in order to avoid a disruptive presence within the group.
- The netnographer must consider ethics and seek, where possible, to protect participant anonymity. This can be particularly challenging considering names and transcripts can be searched for online. Pseudonyms and not quoting publicly available online text verbatim are ways in which to protect anonymity (see Chapter 3).
- Again, ethically, there are several issues with the lurker approach as researchers are observing and investigating online groups without their consent (see Chapter 3).

Methodologically, researchers must justify their approach, but generally there is no perfect or fool-proof method, just methods that are better suited to answer the set question. If you are inclined to use netnography within your research project, carefully consider your research aim(s) and objectives and ask yourself whether netnography is the best approach in helping you gather the type of data you wish to generate.

Group activity

Five example research questions are listed below. In small groups, discuss whether you would use netnography to help answer the proposed research questions.

1 How do university sports societies develop a sense of belonging among their members?

2   In what ways do Major League Baseball (MLB) clubs build brand loyalty?

3   To what extent has fan racism in the National Football League (NFL) shifted from inside the stadium to online spaces?

4   In what ways do athletes use social media platforms to promote themselves?

5   To what extent does 'trash talk' play a role in the participation of online sports gaming?

Discussion points

If you choose to use netnography, which approach might you take? How long would you spend observing? How might you capture your field notes? Would you incorporate any other methods? Are there any limitations of your research approach? You may decide to avoid netnography, if so, which other methods would you employ and why?

Tips and advice

For those who are interested in conducting a netnography, we would recommend the following top ten tips.

(1)   Ensure that you are proficient with the *IT software* and have conducted significant research into the platform in which you are using.

(2)   Enter the community with a *focus* which is directly related to your research aims. Avoid, where possible, preconceptions as these may cloud your judgement. For example, do not enter a football fan forum preconceiving that members are sexist because you will then search for this to potentially prove your preconception. As a researcher, you must keep an open mind.

(3)   From the outset, it is important that you are clear on your research *positionality*, i.e. lurking, partial disclosure, full disclosure, participatory. You should methodologically justify why you adopted your approach.

(4)   *Invest time* within the field, regardless of your positionality. To fully generate rich and quality data, whereby group behaviour is fully understood, interpreted, and critically analysed, immersion is essential.

(5)   *Rapport* is essential for partial, full, and participatory researchers. Ryen (2011: 431) comments that it is 'common knowledge' that 'good rapport . . . may invite participants to disclose emotional experiences'. If we

are probing to uncover experiences of online racism or sexism, for example, better rapport would arguably help participants divulge such personal and emotional stories. As outlined by Deacon et al. (1999: 67), 'all questioning in research depends on winning and maintaining consent' as the researcher has 'to persuade people to co-operate by convincing them of the value of their contribution and of the research as a whole'.

(6) As surprising as this may sound, you must sometimes *act incompetent*. Ethnography and netnography is about understanding the banal, everyday situations in which cultures operate, mutate, and develop. This is perhaps easier for outsider researchers. Netnographers must question the obvious and common-sense, especially during the early stages of the fieldwork as things will be explained to you.

(7) It is important to *stay alert* as you never know when essential data may arise. This is a key skill as there may be long stretches of time where mundane or uninformative conversations are taking place. 'What might at first seem banal could turn out to be pivotal' (Boellstorff et al., 2012: 81).

(8) *Stay critical* of everything. As a researcher, you must question everything you observe. And, question all the information and answers you receive. For instance, although gatekeepers are important, they may lie, embellish the truth, restrict your access, or have an agenda. Moreover, be aware that for some online group members their honesty might be compromised as they may perceive cyberspace to be a 'game', thus possessing an online alter-ego or alias (Farrington et al., 2015).

(9) *Overwrite field notes.* It is always better to have too much data than not enough. Therefore, condition yourself to over-annotate while in the field, especially in the early stages of data collection.

(10) *Be reflexive.* Always consider your role and impact on the research. Be reflexive in your field notes and comprehend how you can limit your bias and influence from the outset.

A word on ethics

Researchers must be fully aware of ethics throughout the research process (see Chapter 3). When conducting a netnography, researchers should consider a number of key questions:

- Is the participant protected from physical, emotional, and psychological harm? Will they be afforded anonymity? Is any data protected?
- Can anyone truly be anonymous online when posting on indexed searchable webpages? If they cannot, what should be done?

- Should participants have to sign a consent form? If so, to what extent does online security issues affect informed consent?
- Is the lurker position ethical? Why might it be sometimes justified? When might it not be acceptable?
- Is it acceptable to deceive online? What scenarios represent online deception?

Although most internet websites are part of the public domain, such as social media sites, and are therefore perfectly valid spaces of investigation, researchers may choose to provide users with anonymity by using pseudonyms. This approach is usually used by lurkers as participants have not provided their consent or where sensitive topics are being explored. Researchers may also wish to paraphrase such online comments as verbatim quotes might be easily located through online search engines. This is always a judgement call by the researcher though as discretion is used to 'decide whether or not the participants have a reasonable expectation of privacy' (Bundon, 2016: 364). Participants who use hashtags, for example, are less likely to have their comments paraphrased as hashtags are specifically used to reach wider audiences. Moreover, famous athletes and celebrities are also less likely to receive anonymity and paraphrasing as they may be followed by thousands, or millions, of people making these steps potentially redundant.

Conclusion

This chapter has explored a variety of key aspects regarding netnography. It has contextualised the discussion by providing important background information on ethnography, the approach that pre-dated netnography. Various forms and approaches to ethnography and netnography have been explained and the connections between them have been highlighted. We discussed the length of time researchers spend within the field and noted that it is often project dependent. While some researchers spend little time, which suits short-term research projects, other researchers devote years to critically investigating online communities. For short-term research projects, which may suit undergraduate students in particular, opportunistic research may arguably be the most appropriate approach. Regardless of whether we are known to the online community we are studying or not, researchers must, from the outset, be clear on their positionality concerning how they intend to enter the online community. While immersed within the field, field notes become an integral part of the research process, and the chapter therefore puts forward the various ways in which field notes can be collected. Because netnography is a highly subjective process, which of course encapsulates field notes, we must remain reflexive at all stages of the research and consider the ways that we interpret and analyse online communication.

Netnography might not suit every research question that focuses on investigating online communities. Instead, a researcher might decide to conduct a content analysis, conduct an online survey, or hold an online focus group to probe further into the phenomenon. Arguably, these approaches are much less time consuming. What netnography does offer, however, is a deeper methodological approach that aims to generate a critical understanding of how online groups mobilise, communicate, and behave. When designing an online study, researchers must ask themselves whether a netnographic approach can unlock richer and more comprehensive data than other available methods. We ask potential netnographic researchers to carefully consider your research aim(s) and objectives and question whether netnography would allow you to achieve these set goals to a deeper and more comprehensive level. If the answer is yes, then we recommend using netnography within your research project.

References

Abeza, G., O'Reilly, N., Seguin, B. and Nzindukiyimana, O. (2017) 'Social media as a relationship marketing tool in professional sport: A netnographical exploration'. *International Journal of Sport Communication*, 10 (3): 325–358.

Adler, P. and Adler, P. (1994) 'Observational techniques'. In Denzin, N. and Lincoln, Y. (Eds.) *Handbook of Qualitative Research*. Thousand Oaks, CA: Sage Publications, pp. 377–392.

Anderson, L. (2006) 'Analytic autoethnography'. *Journal of Contemporary Ethnography*, 35 (4): 373–395.

Armstrong, G. (1998) *Blade Runners: Lives in Football*. Sheffield: The Hallamshire Press.

Atkinson, M. (2016) 'Ethnography'. In Smith, B. and Sparkes, A.C. (Eds.) *Routledge Handbook of Qualitative Research in Sport and Exercise*. New York, NY: Routledge, pp. 49–61.

Boellstorff, T., Nardi, B., Pearce, C. and Taylor, T.L. (2012) *Ethnography and Virtual Worlds: A Handbook of Method*. Princeton, NJ: Princeton University Press.

Bundon, A. (2016) 'The Web and digital qualitative methods: Researching online and researching the online in sport and exercise studies'. In Smith, B. and Sparkes, A.C. (Eds.) *Routledge Handbook of Qualitative Research in Sport and Exercise*. New York, NY: Routledge, pp. 355–367.

Burdsey, D. (2007) *British Asians and Football: Culture, Identity, Exclusion*. Oxon: Routledge.

Cleland, J. and Cashmore, E. (2016) 'Football fans' views of racism in British football'. *International Review for the Sociology of Sport*, 51 (1): 27–43.

Deacon, D., Pickering, M., Golding, P. and Murdock, G. (1999) *Researching Communications: A Practical Guide to Methods in Media and Cultural Analysis*. London: Hodder Arnold.

Farrington, N., Kilvington, D., Price, J. and Saeed, A. (2015) *Sport, Racism and Social Media*. London: Routledge.

Gaiser, T.J. and Schreiner, A.E. (2009) *A Guide to Conducting Online Research*. London: Sage Publications.

Giulianotti, R. (1995) 'Participant observation and research into football hooliganism: Reflections on the problems of entree and everyday risks'. *Sociology of Sport Journal*, 12 (1): 1–20.

Gratton, C. and Jones, I. (2014) *Research Methods for Sports Studies* (3rd Edition). London: Routledge.

Hambrick, M.E. and Kang, S.J. (2014) 'Pin it: Exploring how professional sports organizations use Pinterest as a communications and relationship-marketing tool'. *Communication & Sport*. Available at: https://doi.org/10.1177/2167479513518044

Hine, C. (2012) *The Internet*. Oxford: Oxford University Press.

Holt, N. and Sparkes, A. (2001) 'An ethnographic study of cohesiveness in a college team over a season'. *The Sport Psychologist*, 15 (3): 237–259.

Hynes, D. and Cook, A.M. (2013) 'Online belongings: Female fan experiences in online soccer forums'. In Hutchins, B. and Rowe, D. (Eds.) *Digital Media Sport: Technology, Power and Culture in the Network Society*. New York, NY: Routledge, pp. 97–110.

Kilvington, D. and Price, J. (2017) 'Tackling social media abuse? Critically assessing English football's response to online racism'. *Communication & Sport*. Available at: https://doi.org/10.1177/2167479517745300

Kilvington, D. and Price, J. (2019) 'From backstage to frontstage: Exploring football and the growing problem of online abuse'. In Lawrence, S. and Crawford, G. (Eds.) *Digital Football Cultures Fandom, Identities and Resistance*. London: Routledge, pp. 69–85.

Kozinets, R. (2006) 'Netnography 2.0'. In Belk, R. (Ed.) *Handbook of Qualitative Research Methods in Marketing*. Cheltenham: Edward Elgar Publishing Limited, pp. 129–142.

McNeil, P. and Chapman, S. (2005) *Research Methods* (3rd Edition). New York, NY: Routledge.

Norstedt, M. and Paulsen, J. (2016) 'Moving beyond everyday life in institutional ethnographies: Methodological challenges and ethical dilemmas'. *Qualitative Social Research*, 17 (2): 1–15.

Numerato, D. (2015) 'Behind the digital curtain: Ethnography, football fan activism and social change'. *Qualitative Research*, 16 (5): 575–591.

Pink, S. (2015) *Doing Sensory Ethnography* (2nd Edition). London: Sage Publications.

Pollner, M. and Emerson, R.M. (2001) 'Ethnomethodology and ethnography'. In Atkinson, P., Delamont, S., Coffey, A., Lofland, J. and Lofland, L. (Eds.) *Handbook of Ethnography*. London: Sage Publications, pp. 118–135.

Ryen, A. (2011) 'Ethics and Qualitative Research'. In Silverman, D. (Ed.) *Qualitative Research* (3rd Edition). London: SAGE, pp. 416–438.

Salmons, J. (2016) *Doing Qualitative Research Online*. London: Sage Publications.

Schinke, R.J. and Blodgett, A. (2016) 'Embarking on community-based participatory action research: A methodology that emerges from (and in) communities'. In Smith, B. and Sparkes, A.C. (Eds.) *Routledge Handbook of Qualitative Research in Sport and Exercise*. New York, NY: Routledge, pp. 88–100.

Smith, B. (2013) 'Disability, sport and men's narratives of health: A qualitative study'. *Health Psychology*, 32 (1): 110–119.

Sugden, J. (1996) *Boxing and Society*. Manchester: Manchester University Press.

Thorpe, H. and Olive, R. (2016) 'Conducting observations in sport and exercise settings'. In Smith, B. and Sparkes, A.C. (Eds.) *Routledge Handbook of Qualitative Research in Sport and Exercise*. New York, NY: Routledge, pp. 124–138.

Thrift, N. (2007) *Non-Representational Theory: Space, Politics, Affect*. London: Routledge.

VanDeVen, A.H. (2007) *Engaged Scholarship*. Oxford: Oxford University Press.

Villegas, D. (2018) 'From the self to the screen: A journey guide for auto-netnography in online communities'. *Journal of Marketing Management*, 34 (3–4): 243–262.

Wallace-McRee, L. and Lee, J.W. (2016) 'I like it: Examining NFL Facebook communication strategies'. *Journal of Contemporary Athletics*, 10 (4): 257–276.

7

ANALYSING AND PRESENTING DATA

This chapter focuses attention on the latter stages of a research project. It begins by introducing the concept of analysis and explains why it is important to follow a logical and rigorous process that will help to bring meaning to the data set. It acknowledges differences between quantitative and qualitative analysis and explores key issues relating to each analysis type. For instance, it recognises that there are different types of quantitative data (e.g. nominal, ordinal, interval, and ratio) and discusses the analysis options associated with each of these. Thereafter, the chapter introduces the benefits and limitations associated with qualitative data analysis. Generic stages in the process of qualitative data analysis are then explored before focusing on specific types of analysis processes including content and discourse analysis, interpretative phenomenological analysis, narrative analysis, thematic analysis, and grounded theory. Finally, the chapter concludes with advice for writing up a research project.

KEY POINTS OF THE CHAPTER

- Understand what data analysis means.
- Recognise different forms of quantitative data.
- Know when to use parametric and non-parametric data analysis tests.
- Distinguish between quantitative and qualitative data analysis.
- Appreciate the general stages of qualitative data analysis.
- Show awareness of specific data analysis techniques.

What does analysis mean?

When researchers talk about analysis, they are referring to the process of breaking a complex topic, data, or substance into smaller parts in order to gain a better understanding of it. This involves summarising the data and presenting the results in a way that communicates the most important features. This process is crucial to the generation of knowledge. Think about it: If you do not systematically break the research down into a manageable framework how could you be sure what you have found out and what your contribution to knowledge is? How could you explain your findings to other researchers or your examiners with any conviction? How could you disseminate the research into the mainstream to inform policy and practice? The most obvious answer is with great difficulty.

Over the course of history, methods have been devised to help researchers analyse data efficiently, effectively, and with high **validity**. To say that a form of measurement or analysis is valid, is to say that the analysis tool or system measures what it claims to measure and that the conclusions reached are well founded and are likely to correspond accurately to the proposed setting.

There is an abundance of choice when it comes to methods of analysis. Generally speaking, however, all research analysis is connected to two general themes that correspond to data type. Here we are referring to: (1) Quantitative research methods, which is the systematic investigation of observable phenomena via statistical or mathematical techniques. The goal of which is to develop statistical models to test hypotheses relating to phenomena under study; and (2) Qualitative research methods, which is a scientific method of observation to gather non-numerical data. Its goal is to answer questions as to why and how certain phenomena may occur, rather than how often.

Notwithstanding this, the art of research (quantitative or qualitative) is in selecting and designing a way of approaching your subject area that allows you, not only to observe, but to explain, understand, and interpret. The reasons for analysis can take many forms. Measuring, making comparisons, examining relationships, making forecasts, testing hypotheses, exploring trends, explaining, constructing concepts and theories, and more besides. These are all legitimate reasons for analysis. Whatever the focus, whether you use quantitative or qualitative methods, the process of analysing data is the same, figuratively speaking. Researchers begin by **coding** or labelling the output. They do this as a means to organise the data to make it possible to detect similarities or differences between participants or data sets. Where there are differences we can use various techniques to explain why variances occur. For example, are the differences within a data set correlated with age, sex, height, weight, diet, profession, or other aspects that the research may choose to measure? Where there are commonalities, themes emerge through our data to help us to explain the phenomena under investigation.

Quantitative research

Quantitative researchers use research techniques that summarise numbers so that we can understand their significance to specific samples and/or populations (a population is the largest collection of items that we are interested to study, and the sample is a subset of the population). Data can take different forms (i.e. it can be nominal, ordinal, interval, or ratio) and those different forms dictate the choice of analysis for a researcher.

Nominal and ordinal data

If you have **nominal** data, that means that you are able to assign labels to your data, but the labels do not have any meaningful quantitative value. Suppose for example, you conducted a short survey to find out why prospective students are attracted to the range of courses available within sport studies and you create a list of possible responses based on focus group interviews with a sample of former students who have studied sport. From your initial consultation, you provide a choice of answers for participants to tick, if the choice resonates with them. For analysis purposes, you decide to code the responses in advance.

EXAMPLE

I love sport	= 1
I want to be a sports coach	= 2
I have a thirst for knowledge	= 3
I think health and exercise are important	= 4
I want to be a PE teacher	= 5

The coded answers to the survey are input into a computer to count the frequency of students who enrolled on sports courses because they were aiming to become PE teachers versus those who were seeking employment as sports analysts, versus those who had a thirst for knowledge, and so on. This data is *nominal*.

For data to be categorised as **ordinal** it must feature an orderly scale. Unlike the nominal data example above, the order of the values is important and yet, the differences between each one is not known with significant degrees of confidence. In sport studies settings ordinal data can feature as, for example, Likert scale answers to questionnaires that measure perspective. Suppose you presented the following statement for consideration in an online survey: Transgender athletes should be allowed to compete in sport within their chosen sex category. You offer the following answers for participants to choose from: 'strongly agree', 'agree', 'neither agree or disagree', 'disagree', and 'strongly disagree'. The order of the values is clear but the spacing between categories is unknown. Consequently, this data is ordinal.

Results from research featuring nominal and ordinal data can be cross tabulated with answers to other questions as well as the demographic data in order to find patterns in the responses. Researchers can create graphs, charts, and conduct contingency tables in order to present data to the reader. Simple descriptive statistics, like these, will satisfy some research questions, though in other cases they provide the base for further analysis.

Non-parametric tests

When your data is nominal or ordinal and you are seeking to use **inferential statistics** to make inferences about your sample to a larger population, it is likely that you will need to use non-parametric tests. This is because data measured by nominal or ordinal methods is not expected to be organised in a typical curve form (Thomas, Nelson, and Silverman, 2015). Non-parametric tests are otherwise known as distribution free tests as they do not assume that your data is 'normally distributed'. **Normal distribution** is a statistical feature that tells you how closely all of your data points are gathered around the mean value in the data set.

REMINDER

Mean	The average value within a data set.
Median	The middle value of a data set.
Mode	The value in a data set that occurs most often.

If data is not normally distributed, then our options for applying statistical analysis to the data set are reduced. Thus, it is common to use non-parametric tests when data is nominal or ordinal, as few assumptions can be made about the data, or when samples are taken from several different populations. It is true that non-parametric tests are less statistically powerful than parametric tests and that they need larger sample sizes to generate the same level of significance. Table 7.1 below provides an example of some non-parametric tests that are available to sport studies researchers:

TABLE 7.1 Non-Parametric Tests

Name	*What is it used for?*
Komogarov–Smirnov	Attempts to determine if two data sets differ significantly.
Mann–Whitney U Test	Non-parametric equivalent of the t-test but does not require the assumption of normal distribution. Used to determine whether two independent samples were selected from populations with the same distribution.
Kendall Rank Correlation Coefficient	Measures the ordinal association between two measured quantities.

(Continued)

TABLE 7.1 (Continued)

Name	What is it used for?
Kruskal–Wallis test	Otherwise known as the one-way ANOVA on ranks is a non-parametric method for testing whether samples originate from the same distribution. It is used to compare two or more independent samples.
Cramer Coefficient	Measures the association of variables with nominal categories.

Interval and ratio data

Interval data shares similarities with ordinal level data, with one characteristic setting it apart: That the intervals between the variables are equally spaced. In other words, data is interval when we know the order and exact differences between values. Suppose you are measuring distance jumped in a long jump competition. Participant one jumps 2 m and 32 cm, participant two jumps 2 m and 28 cm, and participant three jumps 2 m and 24 cm. The first participant jumps 4 cm further than the second, and the second jumps 4 cm more than the third. Thus, because interval scales tell us about the order and also about the value between each variable there are more opportunities to measure tendency in the form of mode, median, mean, and standard deviation (note: **Standard Deviation** measures how far each variable within a data set varies from the mean value). It is worth noting that interval data does not have a true zero in the sense that zero and minus numbers can also feature as measurements on a sliding scale.

By contrast, whilst everything about interval data applies to ratio data too, there is one exception. **Ratio data** has a clear definition of zero and it is this feature that opens up the fullest range of possibilities when it comes to statistical analysis. This is because interval and ratio data often (but not always) meet the criteria for the use of **parametric** statistical tests. Researchers can use parametric tests if the data satisfies the assumptions of normal distribution, homogeneity of variance, linearity, and independence. Given that parametric tests (see Table 7.2) are largely assumed to hold greater statistical power, they tend to be the most preferred types of tests used within sport studies.

One of the most common uses of parametric statistics in sport studies occurs when researchers set out to measure differences within or across data groups. When researchers set out to search for difference of this type, they can apply an analysis of variance, otherwise known as an ANOVA. Suppose, for example, you are interested in determining the relative intelligence levels of different communities of sportsmen and women. Having administered an online IQ test for athletes to complete, you input the data from the hockey team, soccer team, baseball team, and rugby team into Statistical Package for Social Sciences (Note: **SPSS** is a statistical

TABLE 7.2 Parametric Tests

Name	What is it used for?
Pearson's correlation coefficient	Examines the relationship between interval and ratio variables.
Spearman's Rho	Examines correlation when both variables are ordinal or when one is ordinal and the other is interval/ratio.
Chi Square Test	Measures the degree of association between two variables.
One Group T-Test	Compares the means of the results from the sample compared with the population mean.
One-way Analysis of Variance	Tests the difference between means of results gained under different conditions.
Multiple Regression	Measures the effects of two or more independent variables on a single dependent variable measured on interval or ratio scales.
Logistic Regression	Development of multiple regression that can hold certain variables constant in order to assess the independent influence of key variables of interest.
Factor Analysis	Used to examine the relationship between latent (unobserved) and observed variables. It packages information for data reduction. Variables that correlate with each other are combined to create a super-variable. Clusters of variables are reduced to a factor.

software programme that makes running statistical tests more time efficient). You could use an ANOVA to determine if the mean IQ level is significantly different across groups, thus identifying which group is the smartest. (Note: Researchers conduct an ANOVA when they are looking to determine whether two or more groups differ significantly on a specific measure or test).

Rather than looking for differences between or within groups on singular occasions or across time via repeated measures, sport studies researchers may also be looking for sophisticated ways to predict an outcome. Suppose for example, you are looking to predict the outcome of men and women's England matches at the soccer World Cup. Of course, we can carry out this procedure in layman form (meaning without professional or specialised knowledge) often with varying degrees of success. When we make an educated guess on the outcome of matches, we are applying a crude form of quantitative analysis. We do this by thinking about the historic results between the teams (do England usually beat Brazil?), the climate (is it too hot for English players?), the managers (what strategy are they likely to employ?), the players (do certain English attackers like playing against certain defensive opponents?). In other words, we use our knowledge from the past to predict the future. The statistical technique, **multiple regression analysis** applies this very process in a sophisticated way using statistics. The key is to provide consistent and reliable data on the past performance of both teams and players and then allow the statistics to provide a prediction within confidence levels. Of course, there are many more statistical analytical possibilities, some of which were outlined in Table 7.2 above. For further details on these and numerous other quantitative analysis procedures relevant to the study of sport-related topics please see Gratton and Jones (2015).

Individual activity

Download one sport-related study via an appropriate search platform (such as the library catalogue at your university or Google Scholar) that has used parametric data analysis techniques, and another that has used non-parametric data techniques (these can be searched through terms like 'parametric test sport' and 'non-parametric test sport'). Discuss the strengths and limitations of the study's conclusions with a classmate or colleague.

Qualitative data analysis

In qualitative data analysis, words and or pictures rather than numbers, are the focus of analysis. When implementing methods that feature human participants every effort is made to provide participants with a space in which they can express their views, elaborate their theories, and share their perspectives. Whether conducting online interviews, surveys, ethnographic work, and more options besides, qualitative research focuses attention at the level of the individual, site/space, or culture under investigation. This occurs within the canopy of anonymity and the knowledge that participant thoughts will be taken seriously and analysed appropriately. The hallmark of qualitative research is its emphasis on interpretation.

Researchers must find a way of identifying and labelling themes that appear in the text of a transcript. Given that data is presented in the form of text and that the methods employed are more likely to emphasise **inductive** rather than **deductive** design, pre-coding is not always possible or desirable. To say that research is inductive means that researchers analyse the data free from preconceived ideas, hypotheses, or theories, and that findings are driven by the data in an attempt to use observations to find patterns and to create theory, rather than test it.

The inductive nature of some qualitative research often lends itself to a more fluid process when compared with the tightly controlled procedures that are a feature of quantitative analysis. Nonetheless, there are commonalities in the stages of qualitative analysis across approaches. Later in this chapter we dedicate space to discuss and display examples of specific analysis types, but first let us remind ourselves of those generic stages of qualitative analysis that feature across methods.

General stages in qualitative analysis

A vast amount of data can be generated during a qualitative research project. Consequently, this must be managed through the analysis process. It is the researcher's job to organise the data in such a way that he or she can bring insight and meaning to the data set. To do this in a systematic manner, researchers will follow specific analysis methods that relate specifically to the aim(s) and objectives of the project. Notwithstanding this, in the section below we describe those general stages of the analysis process that are associated with most (not all) qualitative studies.

Transcription

Most qualitative research studies require some type of transcription. For example, if you are recording interviews, focus groups, advertisements, or sports commentary, it is important that you have an accurate account of the content. Transcription is the process of writing down exactly what people say and do and the context in which they do it. To say that something has been transcribed verbatim means that it has been recorded in written form word for word. Of course, if you are conducting your research digitally via text message, on chat rooms, via online surveys, or by other electronic communications, then transcription has already taken place. That is one of the time-saving advantages of research in the internet era. But, let us presume that you are responsible for providing a digital version by inputting the data. Some tips include:

(1) Anonymise sensitive data. All personally identifiable features should be removed from the data.
(2) Use abbreviations where possible. This will save time, but do not forget to keep a list to remind you what those abbreviations mean. This will be useful when you revisit the data in the months to come.
(3) Try to capture the emotion of any exchanges. If interviews have been streamed via synchronous visual methods (e.g. Skype) make notes in brackets (laughing, crying, smiling).
(4) When formatting the transcript, use double line spacing and give yourself generous margins. This will be useful for making notes on the transcripts in preparation for the generation of codes.

Immersion and familiarisation

If you are the person responsible for transcribing the data, then you will (as a result of transcription) already be familiar with the text. Transcription offers the perfect opportunity to get to know your data. If you have conducted the interview yourself, you might expect to have a good grasp of the data. But when you transcribe the data retrospectively, aspects are revealed to you that reach beyond your initial expectations. You will be surprised how much more relevant information is available. If, however, you have not seen the data until this point, then to get a feel for the perspectives, views, and experiences of the participants it is crucial that you read and re-read the transcription to become familiar with people, events, and quotations that sit together. If time allows, it is also a good idea to listen to the interviews again. This will help the researcher to gain an understanding of the emotive delivery of quotations, the humour, sarcasm, and wit that can get lost on the printed page. A thorough analytic process demands heightened awareness of the data.

First stage coding

Once you are familiar with the data, it is time to attempt to organise it into codes. According to Saldana (2016), a code in qualitative inquiry is often a word or short phrase that symbolically assigns a summative, salient, essence capturing, and/or evocative attribute for a portion of language-based or visual data. In other words, whatever material you are working with (be it an interview transcript, qualitative survey response, field notes, media stories, and more besides) there will be commonalities in the data (i.e. shared characteristics) between participants or qualitative instances. Codes record such instances.

Marshall and Rossman (2006: 159) remind researchers that the process of identifying salient themes that link aspects of data together is the most intellectually challenging phase of data analysis. They argue that 'the researcher generates categories through prolonged engagement with the data', and that, these categories then become 'buckets or baskets into which segments of text are placed'. So, when creating your 'buckets', or developing preliminary coding, ask yourself the following questions: What is the data telling you? Anything obvious? What are the dominant issues from individual participants? What are the dominant issues between participants? Are there any potential theoretical leads? To help with this, consider the following example:

RESEARCHER: Tell me how you started taking part in the sport of cage fighting.

PARTICIPANT 1: Well, I was what they call a **'Tomboy'** at school. When the other girls were skipping and playing with dolls I was joining in with the football and other boy's stuff. I was known for being tough, not a fighter, but a competitor. Whatever I did, I was going to win.

PARTICIPANT 2: I was always a fighter. My dad said I would fight with myself in an empty room. My mum is similar to me. We are both **Tomboy's**, much more comfortable in men's company and suited to the harsh training of stereotypical men's sports. It's my mum that took me to my first mixed martial arts class.

In this short extract, it is reasonable to assume that issues relating to the concept 'Tomboy' should feature as a provisional code. Whilst this code is likely to be modified later, it is an important first step in categorising the data. Remember, qualitative researchers use the coding process in order to gather an aggregate of similar instances so that the researcher can work with them all together, allowing researchers to gain an insight of the data. It is worth noting here that as the researcher codes the data, new understandings may emerge. As a qualitative researcher it is important to remain flexible and allow the data to take you in new directions.

Individual activity

Choose a story concerning sport in any major news media outlet today (print newspaper, online newspaper, major broadcaster such as the BBC, NBC, AP, Reuters, CNN, ABC News, that you can access online). Using our guidance in this section of the chapter, start to work through it, identifying first stage codes that can then be taken into second stage codes and then into recurring themes that can be presented in the analysis section of a research project (covered later in this section of the chapter).

Keep memos

Keeping **memos** or a research diary is a good idea to accompany your research project. Memos are informal records that are held by the research team to help them to shape their ideas. They are there to catch your ideas either digitally or on paper before they disappear from your brain. We all have moments of clarity when we are going about our daily routines. Our mistake is often to think that we will clearly recall those thoughts at a later date. Keeping memos is a strategy to counter the fallibility of human memory by recording key thoughts.

TIPS

- Date every entry.
- Write each entry in the first person (i.e. from the researcher's point of view or perspective).
- Do not worry about writing style (memo's are for your eyes only).
- Be as vivid as possible to help with memory recall later in the process.
- Leave a note to explain how this memo will be valuable to the project or what concerns you have, if any.

Second stage coding

Richards (2015) reminds us that the main purpose of qualitative coding is about data retention, not data reduction. She means that processes must be put in place to reduce the data whilst simultaneously representing all of it. The goal is to keep revisiting the data until you understand the patterns and explanations for them. Thus, coding is not merely a process of labelling. It is a process that helps you to think about patterns in the data and the relationships within or between them.

At the second stage of coding the researchers must build on the open coding process (stage one) that preceded it. All derived categories should be internally consistent but distinct from other categories. So, of the codes that you developed at stage one, are there any connections between them? Perhaps it is possible for one code to subsume another if the code description is slightly altered. For example, let us presume that you had the following codes from the stage one example we raised above.

---

(1) Tomboy (a self-described phenomenon and the context in which it arises).
(2) Challenging gendered stereotypes (interactions that stem from it).
(3) Coping with negativity in masculine environments (consequences and implications for the individual).

You might decide to combine these codes from stage one in order to broaden conceptual explanations that are offered across participants and data sets. This means expanding the code to capture the contextual narrative. In this instance, a new code (or core category) *Gendered Stigma* could be used to encompass the stage one codes in order to offer a multi-layered, information rich, complex account of related concepts within the participant's journey. This new code can then be validated against the data.

Saturation

The coding process does not always precede in an orderly fashion. It can be messy and time consuming. The objective is to bring order to a mass of data that would otherwise lack coherence. Through the coding process, commonalities and differences in the data are noted in order to create conceptual scaffolding for interpretation. But how do you know when to stop coding, after all, you could go on and on. The answer is that you stop once the point of saturation has been reached. Practically and theoretically speaking, you have reached the point of saturation once no new categories or themes can be derived from the data. If each new data extract can be included into the existing themes, you have reached the point of saturation.

Interpreting codes, categories, and themes

Themes are the outcome of coding and emerge through the process of coding and interpretation. At this point the researchers job becomes more complex. Listing themes is all well and good, but what do they mean? What do they tell us about the phenomenon under investigation? What do they add to the research narrative? What explanations can you offer? What conclusions can be drawn? What inferences can be made? And what are the implications of your findings? When seeking answers to those questions it is important that the researcher considers three main issues: (1) Has the researcher critically examined their own role, potential bias, and influence during each stage of the research process; (2) Has the researcher acknowledged other plausible explanations; and (3) Where there are outliers to the categorised themes (i.e. a small number of observations that are distant or conceptually diverse to the dominant themes), has the researcher acknowledged them? Ultimately, it is interpretation that brings meaning and coherence to the identified themes and patterns.

Ensuring rigour

Some criticisms given to qualitative studies are that the findings are anecdotal (implying that qualitative researchers are not 'scientific' enough), sample sizes are often (but not always) small, methods are not heavily controlled and therefore largely unrepeatable, the evidence is not generalisable and the researcher could have interpreted the data in more than one way. There are, of course, counter claims in the sense that:

- Comprehensive data treatment (all cases in qualitative research are incorporated into the analysis) go beyond what is demanded in quantitative methods.
- Heavily controlled studies (experiments) are not appropriate for certain forms of knowledge generation.
- Repeatability of method is not always desirable.
- Small sample sizes produce an abundance of rich meaningful data.
- Generalisable theories are too simplistic to explain complex phenomena.
- Possible variations in interpretation are just as apparent for quantitative as they are for qualitative researchers.

Nevertheless, there are procedures that can be put in place to help ensure that the **rigour** of qualitative research is as good as it could be. **Triangulation** involves the analysis of multiple methods of data collection to produce a more accurate and objective interpretation of the data. The idea is to say that if the results of a social survey reveal similar results to interviews or media portrayals of a specific phenomenon, then the findings have more explanatory power. Whilst plausible, this is contested by some researchers who argue that it is optimistic at best to believe that the aggravation of data from different sources will necessarily produce a more complete picture. Denzin and Lincoln (2018) argue that triangulation is not a means to obtain a 'true' reading. Instead, it should be understood as a strategy to add rigour, breadth, complexity, and depth to any research project.

Respondent Validation can also be useful. This is the process in which researchers take their interpretation of results back to the respondents in order to validate the findings. Using this process, tentative results can be altered in response to the feedback from the participants. This helps to ensure (as far as possible) that the findings are representative of the group that the researcher seeks to understand.

Group activity

Stage 1: In class, record a 5-minute interview with a colleague about their experiences of sport participation. Find out as much as possible about when and why participation began, how it progressed, and the barriers that they have faced on their journey.

Stage 2: Transcribe this short interview in your own time verbatim (word for word).

Stage 3: Work with a partner to code the data (taking into consideration the detail in the section above).

Stage 4: What are the dominant themes from the interview? (Provide an example from the data for each theme).

Stage 5: Discuss the potential links of those themes to literature/theory.

Stage 6: Report back on your experience.

Specific forms of qualitative analysis

Let us remind ourselves of some of the analysis types that are available to qualitative researchers. It is important to remember that just as a statistical computer package such as SPSS will not tell you which tests to run and why, there is no computer package to inform you which qualitative analysis methods are most appropriate to use either. Below we highlight a few options.

Content analysis

According to Cohen, Manion, and Morrison (2002), content analysis was originally established as a means to transform verbal, non-quantitative documents into quantitative data. Akin to quantitative analysis, the word count and numerical categorisations are developed from the data. Content analysis researchers must follow bespoke but strict protocol in order to ensure the reliability of this data analysis method. For Gray (2018), the key to successfully conducting content analysis is to follow procedures that ensure that patterns of communication are analysed in a replicable and systematic manner.

Research in sport

'An examination of how alcohol brands use sport to engage consumers on social media', by Westberg et al. (2018).

What was the aim of the research?

The research had one specific aim: To understand how alcohol brands were using the intersection of sport and social media, and consumers identification with sport, to further their marketing goals.

What were the methods used?

A qualitative content analysis was adopted to examine the social media activity of alcohol brands that were sponsors of the three largest spectator sports in Australia (Australian Rules Football, rugby league, and cricket). Social media platforms were thought to facilitate a natural source of data in an accessible and contextual form. Data was captured by accessing the social media sites (Twitter and Facebook) associated with alcohol brands and sporting associations. The researchers implemented simple but effective screen capture technology to record instances, which were then archived. Data analysis considered text and images, as well as the processes via which online communities communicate (i.e. by liking posts). Only the content that pertained to sport was retained. The analysis took an inductive approach to elicit themes from the online texts and images that had been captured. Communications were open coded and then themes were identified.

What were the key findings?

A total of 1,086 brand-authored Facebook and Twitter posts were collected and categorised over the research period. Of these, 236 brand-authored messages were identified as sport linked communication (128 Facebook posts and 108 tweets). The 128 Facebook brand-authored messages generated 46,616 likes, 4,300 comments, and 6,052 shares, thus reflecting high levels of interest. The 108 brand-authored messages on Twitter reflected engagement with 1,202 'favourites' and were associated with 1,045 retweets. Whilst 31 percent (72 posts) were simply noted to be branding communication with no attempt to activate the customer, 69 percent (164 posts) sought to actively engage the customer in *calls to action*, which stimulate customers to actively interact with the brand. Techniques included *call to collaborate* (e.g. encouraging consumers to share content); *call to compete* (by leveraging the competitive nature of sports fans to, for example take part in promotional competitions to win alcohol branded, sport-related prizes); *call to celebrate* (normalising the consumption of alcohol as a way to celebrate sport victory); *call to consume* (positioning alcohol as part of the regular sport fan experience).

This paper highlights the powerful combination of sport and social media as a mechanism to extend the marketing efforts of brands. The use of social media users to promote the brands makes it difficult for regulators to identify and control.

Discourse analysis

Discourse analysis shares similar features to content analysis, but whilst content analysis is concerned with receiving meaningful information from documents in terms of frequencies of key messages, discourse analysis draws attention to the ways that language is used in texts and contexts. To simplify further, content analysis is concerned with content. Discourse analysis is concerned with the use of language within the content or associated meanings or implications. Potter and Wetherell (1987) assert that because discourse analysis aims to gain a better understanding of social life from an examination of texts, it can be said to take a **social constructionist** approach to research.

Broadly speaking, this means that users of discourse analysis often adopt a critical stance towards the taken for granted ways that we understand the world and ourselves. They argue that 'realities' are constructed through social processes and that clues to social processes are bound in our use of linguistics, both spoken and written. For example, the way we use language provides clues as to how we construct our social worlds. It holds a window to identity, how we would like to be perceived, how we perceive others, our public facing attitudes on a wide range of matters. The role of the analysist is to analyse the micro and/or macro constructions to tell us more about the participants or material under study.

Research in sport

'Mother runners in the blogosphere: A discursive psychological analysis of online recreational athlete identities', by McGannon, McMahon and Gonsalves (2016).

What was the aim of the research?

Qualitative research on physically active mothers has shown that recreational sport may allow women to resist good mother ideals that often constrain exercise. Thus, the aim of this study was to extend this understanding in a socio-cultural context by examining how recreational mother identities were constructed within one form of new media – blogging.

What were the methods used?

The North American online running community *Another Mother Runner* was used as the data collection site. Discourse analysis of 30 stories and 177 reader comments and visual data from 102 images (accompanying stories) was conducted. Analytical steps involved: Re-reading blog/postings/stories and reader comments; developing abstract, emergent coding paradigms by highlighting specific words and terms within passages; attaching initial coding paradigms to broader categories based on socio-cultural understandings from the sport psychology literature; linguistic categories were also identified as a means to create new identities. In addition, visual images that were attached to stories were coded to contextualise the discourses taking place.

What were the key findings?

In the findings the researchers identified two primary discourses. First, a discourse of transformation and empowerment was identified where stories were portrayed primarily as a practice that allows women to literally exercise self-identity transformation and mould themselves into runners. Secondly, a discourse of disruption and resolution in that transformation and empowerment was associated with reaching and working through difficult life milestones from which athlete mothers emerged as enlightened and more resilient. Additionally, excerpts revealed how women learned to deal with new disruptions of injury and resolve problems with the aid of online communications.

Interpretive phenomenological analysis (IPA)

Derived from the philosophies of **phenomenology** and **hermeneutics**, IPA is a qualitative method for analysing data in psychology (Phenomenology is the study of perception while hermeneutics is the study of interpretation). IPA differs from other research in psychology in which **nomothetic** research rules. In this context, nomothetic means that psychologists often attempt to find universal laws or similarities between people. They tend to classify people into groups (such as people with disorders), establish common principles (such as behaviourist laws of learning), or establish dimensions (such as Eysenk's personality inventory). IPA is different because it is an **idiographic** mode of inquiry where the focus is on the individual experience, particularly regarding how individuals make sense of their lives and the social structures that they operate within.

Whilst findings cannot create generalisable laws as such, they can add to the evidence base and serve as a hypothesis for future research. According to Smith and Eatough (2007), IPA analysis always begins with the detailed reading of a single case, after which the case can be written up as a case study or else the researcher then moves on to a second case, and so on. The key for analysis, they explain, is to ensure that it should be possible to learn something about important generic themes (assuming that the research involves a group of cases) but emphasis must be placed upon how participants interpret their own lives.

Research in sport

'Athletes' experiences of social support during their transition out of elite sport: An interpretive phenomenological analysis', by Brown et al. (2018).

What was the aim of the research?

The aim of the study was to gain a comprehensive insight into the ways that social support may influence how athletes adjust to life following their retirement from elite sport.

What were the methods used?

IPA was deemed an appropriate method to use as it is suitable for data collection methods that afford participants the opportunity to offer in depth, first person accounts of their experiences. A purposive sample of eight former elite athletes from the UK were recruited through social media and agreed to be interviewed face-to-face (for more on online interviews see Chapter 5). The researchers explored the context, structure, and meaning of participant's experiences. All participants were given pseudonyms to protect confidentiality. Notes were made on the transcripts in three stages. First, by paying close attention to the participant's experiences. Second, an examination of the language that was used by participants, paying attention to the repetition of words, phrases, metaphors, and the way the account was expressed. Third, the researchers examined the accounts on a conceptual level to gain a deeper understanding of the meaning that was attached to what was being discussed. These notes were subsequently used to develop emergent themes, and concomitantly, emergent themes were used to develop superordinate themes (i.e. broader themes encompassing an amalgamation of emergent themes) whilst still retaining the idiographic focus that is central to IPA.

What were the key findings?

Participants described two broad stages of transition. At stage one, which was characterised by feelings of loss, denial, and uncertainty about the future, two superordinate themes were identified (a) *Feeling cared for and understood*, where participants acknowledged that empathy from significant others was the biggest support; b) *Ability to seek and ask for support*, where participants admitted finding it difficult to ask for help and to find new social networks outside of their former career. The second stage of transition was characterised by participants redefining their athletic identity and, in some instances, becoming a supporter of the sport or other athletes. This aided the transition, offering athletes an opportunity to use the knowledge and skills that they had gained to simultaneously help others and themselves.

Narrative analysis

Whilst IPA focuses attention on the ways in which a person views his or her own life and past experiences, **narrative analysis** is concerned with interpreting how a person's life chronology has led them to experience life in various ways. In other words, the process of the lived experience and the social structures that guide the experience are thought to be important factors that determine action. Narratives ordinarily comprise of an entire life story or they are centred around a specific event. As Elliott (2005) explains, narratives do not necessarily provide an account of how life was lived or the exact details of an event (in the same way that contemporary field notes might), but it provides a flavour of what took place. The reflection on actual events holds value by providing meaningful data from the perspective of key informants. Narratives are widely used in the social sciences as a valid method for gathering information for academic research.

Research in sport

'Leave your ego at the door': A Narrative investigation into effective wing-suit flying', by Arijs et al. (2017).

What were the aims of the research?

The aim of this study was to conduct a narrative analysis to investigate the experiences of effective performance in the extreme sport of wingsuit flying, a relatively new parachute sport involving a specially designed jumpsuit that facilitates forward motion and directional control. The researchers contend that because a number of narrative studies have been conducted into the lives of elite sports people and this has led to significant theoretical advancements offering nuanced understandings around performance, lifestyle, and motivation, it was an appropriate area to investigate in the current context. The research literature is growing in relation to 'traditional sports' where the hallmarks of performance narratives include prioritisation of competition, winning, discipline, sacrifice, hard work, technique, the relegation of personal relationships, play, and enjoyment.

What methods were used?

A purposive sample of six elite wingsuit pilots were identified and then contacted via their profiles present on the internet. For reasons of geographical distance from the researchers, interviews were conducted using the communications software Skype. All interviews were recorded and transcribed verbatim. The lead researcher immersed himself in the data by listening to the interviews and reading the transcripts multiple times. Emergent themes were developed, amended, and approved with the input of the wider research team. The identified themes were then sent to the participants for member reflections (otherwise known as **respondent validation**).

What were the key findings?

The findings indicated that wingsuit flying pilot's value alternative qualities (to that of athletes in traditional sports) in the pursuit of performance excellence through the identification of four themes: (1) *Know thy skills*: Much like athletes in traditional sports, participants placed emphasis on skills and technical knowledge. However, an important distinction was that the pilots focused on knowing the limits of their technical skills and capabilities rather than seeking to maximise or push their skills. Given the danger associated with wingsuit pilots, the participants were aware that being in control was a fundamental skill; (2) *Know the environment now*: Being in tune with the environment was important to participants. Whereas performance narratives in traditional sports tend to be positioned in opposition to all obstacles (injury, conditions, competitors), pilots reveal a sense of trying to connect with and co-operate with potential obstacles (weather and other environmental factors); (3) *Tame the 'inner animal'*: Managing the desire to push beyond ones capabilities was noted by participants as a means to preserve safety; 4) *Leave your ego at the door*: To perform optimally the pilot must strike a balance between risk and reward. The pilot must not strike all out for glory but he or she must deliberately retain a margin for error to allow the capacity to resolve unexpected issues. Findings suggest that effective extreme sports participation is not about innate abilities, who can take the biggest risk, or who can demonstrate the most macho line. What counts is continuous self-evaluation, personal restraint, and judgement.

Thematic analysis

Thematic analysis is a common form of analysis in sport studies. This is because whilst other methods are tied to, or have developed from, a particular theoretical or **epistemological** position, thematic analysis is not subject to the same constraints. The method is flexible and it can be used across disciplines and theoretical frameworks. According to Braun and Clarke (2008: 81), 'thematic analysis can be a method to both reflect reality and unpick or unravel the surface of reality'. Thematic analysis can be an **essentialist** method where the experiences, meanings, and reality for participants is emphasised. Equally, Braun and Clarke remind us, it can be a **constructionist** method which examines the way in which events, realities, meanings, and experiences are the effects of a range of discourses operating in society.

Ambiguity, as it applies to thematic analysis does not mean that the procedures are complex or that the underpinning philosophy is difficult to understand. In fact, the premise of thematic analysis is simple: The researcher will identify and analyse patterns (otherwise known as themes) in the data and interpret those themes accordingly. Rice and Ezzy (1999: 258) describe how the process of creating themes occurs 'through careful reading and re-reading of the data'. By immersing oneself in the data set, it is possible to recognise patterns within and across data sets. Themes are often identified if there is reoccurring content across data sets (the data sets share common characteristics), or more simply when it captures something important in relation to the research question.

One of the strengths of thematic analysis is its flexibility to allow researchers to determine themes in a number of ways. For example, themes can be identified inductively, that is to say themes develop from the data and are not influenced from any pre-existing theoretical or empirical preconceptions. In contrast, researchers might decide that theoretical thematic analysis is the best option. In either instance, it is important to be consistent in your approach within any particular analysis.

Research in sport

'Acceptability of a digital health intervention alongside physiotherapy to support patients following anterior cruciate ligament reconstruction', by Dunphy et al. (2017).

What was the aim of the research?

In this study the researchers evaluated the acceptability of TRAK-based blended intervention in post-ACL reconstruction rehabilitation. They interviewed 12 patients recovering from Anterior Crucial Ligament (ACL) reconstructive surgery. The patients were receiving a blended intervention of face-to-face physiotherapy and a digital exercise programme. The latter aspect (web-based tool TRAK) provides individuals with an individually tailored exercise programme with video instructions and progress logs for each exercise, relevant health information, and a contact option which allows each patient to email a physiotherapist for additional support.

What methods were used?

After the participants had been using the TRAK system for four months, semi-structured interviews were conducted to focus on the experience of ACL rehabilitation. All interviews were digitally recorded and then transcribed verbatim by the lead researcher. Data from the interviews was analysed using an inductive form of thematic analysis in which data (rather than theory) was driving the process. Initially, the data was coded by the lead researcher and agreed by another team member. A dialectic process followed until agreement was reached. Themes emerging from the interviews were grouped together until saturation.

What were the key findings?

The findings indicated that patients were generally in favour of the blended approach. The online element helped them to remember instructions from the physiotherapist and the online group provided a support network between the patients. It acted as a prompt to do physical activity, and the videos featuring demonstrations were a trusted source of information, given that they were produced and approved by physiotherapists. However, whilst patients were positive about the inclusion of

> TRAK as part of their rehabilitation journey, they were clear that they did not see this as an alternative to face-to-face physiotherapy appointments. Physiotherapists were also aware of the benefits, but highlighted that organisational changes are needed to better integrate its use into standard physiotherapy practice.

Grounded theory

Where thematic analysis sets out to describe, interpret, and explain a set of behaviours or actions or rhetoric, grounded theory takes this to the next level. Grounded theory is a way of thinking about and conceptualising data and creating theory. The idea emerged from the work of Glaser and Strauss (1967), who explained that when very little is known about the topic under investigation; when there are no grand theories; or when you wish to challenge existing theories and create new ones; then grounded theory is a suitable methodology. Researchers, they argue, ought to rid themselves of preconceptions as much as possible and accept the data at face value.

We have deliberately left grounded theory until last, because it is more than a process of analysis. In his seminal paper on grounded research in sport and exercise psychology, Weed (2009) refers to how grounded theory is a 'total methodology'. He means that the principles of grounded theory must be followed from the conceptualisation of the research issue to the end of the research project (where the product or outcome of the research has been met). The researcher's epistemological position (relating to the perception of the nature of knowledge) will inform the methodology (otherwise to be thought of as the overall research strategy). In turn, this will guide the methods used and the specific tools to collect data. For Weed, there a number of core elements to grounded theory methodology, some of which are briefly outlined below:

> (1) **Iterative process:** Using grounded theory is particularly time intensive because it employs an iterative process. This means that there is more than one stage to data collection and analysis as the objective is to develop theory through carefully designed research stages. The desired outcome becomes closer to discovery with each iteration. In practical terms, in one iteration, data will be collected, analysed, and compared with the literature. Following this, a second iteration begins where further data is collected in an attempt to help to refine concepts from iteration and results are compared with the literature. This leads on to the focused collection of more data until theoretical saturation is reached (see number 6 below).

(2) ***Theoretical Sampling***: At each iteration, researchers will target a sample of the population that they think know most about an issue and therefore can help to develop theory. The theoretical sample is directly informed by the outcome of the last iteration.

(3) ***Theoretical Sensitivity***: It is a mistake to think that those researchers who use grounded theory have little knowledge of the research area. In fact, it is important that researchers are sensitive to and have an awareness of the area. The crucial point is that researchers can be sensitive to the research area without developing preconceived notions about what they might discover.

(4) ***Codes, Memos, and Concepts***: The basic process of grounded theory coding seeks to describe the phenomena before moving to a second stage which seeks to conceptualise the phenomena. The development from description to conceptualisation is facilitated by memo writing in which emergent ideas are formally noted and used to inform the iteration process.

(5) ***Constant Comparison***: Once the analysis has developed beyond the initial stages, the constant comparison between data, codes, concepts, and literature is a strategy for continually checking that the emerging insights are grounded in all parts of the analysis.

(6) ***Theoretical Saturation***: When fresh data no longer offers new theoretical insights, theoretical saturation has been reached.

(7) ***Fit, Work, Relevance, and Modifiability***: Rather than assessing the worth of grounded theory research via means of reliability and validity, researchers talk about fit, work, relevance, and modifiability. Fit relates to how closely the developed theory fits the data. It is ensured in the process of constant comparison and theoretical saturation. The theory works if it can explain the phenomena under investigation and its relevance relates to the extent to which it deals with real concerns of the participants. Finally, given the nature of grounded theory, the theory should be modifiable or open to extension to accommodate new insights.

In sum, grounded theory often involves a fairly continuous iteration between data collection and analysis. It is a time intensive research method which has the potential to unearth deep analysis and theory generation. In today's academic world, where universities are under pressure to generate a high frequency of research outputs in order to reach performance targets, grounded theory is underused.

Constructing a research project

You have accurately conducted the most appropriate method of analysis and you have some interesting findings to share with academic and practice specific audiences. It is time to communicate your findings as effectively as you can. Generally speaking, and certainly for empirical studies, your research should cover a number of sections to ensure that your audience have all relevant and pertinent information available to them. Below we highlight each section and give a brief description of its purpose and the content that is usually included.

The abstract

The abstract of any research paper must provide a clear summary of the research. It is a chance to inform potential readers of all of the important information. Potential readers usually read the abstract of a research paper to get a flavour of the research and then decide whether to read the full article. It is, therefore, important to communicate elements such as the aims and rationale, variables, procedures, analysis, results, conclusions, and implications of your research to the field. Whilst this seems like an exhaustive list, your job is to be as concise as possible.

The introduction

A brief contextual introduction is needed to outline important background information capable of promoting interest. The purpose as well as the rationale for the study should be clearly articulated within this section. The introduction also provides an opportunity to briefly explore the relevance of the study to further the knowledge or evidence base relating to the chosen area as well as identifying the project's aim(s) and objectives.

Literature review

As we discussed in detail in Chapter 2, the literature review is an extension of the introduction as it builds a more detailed picture for the reader. As well as promoting interest it should use the extant literature to contextualise matters. It should discuss literature that is pertinent to the research problem, critiquing theory, methods, and results as it advances. It should draw reference to gaps in the literature (highlighting where more research is needed) as well as critiquing published articles on related topics. You should explain how your project will extend the existing literature and its relevance to the field. This section might end with a reminder of the project's aim(s), supported by a hypothesis where relevant.

The methodological approach

The next stage is to explain what you did and why you decided to do it that way. Within this section, the researcher must demonstrate the appropriateness of the methodology in relation to the research aim(s) and objectives. The reader will be looking for clarity and completeness of procedural description, such that the work could be replicated or used as a framework for other researchers to model future work on. The researcher should demonstrate awareness of ethical issues, particularly in relation to any persons used as participants. They should also justify the appropriateness of the analysis techniques used as well as explaining steps taken towards increasing the validity and reliability of their study.

The results

Not all research projects will need a results section, but where appropriate it should display pertinent data in an effective format (e.g. tables, charts, stats etc.). It is important that there is a clarity and completeness of presentation with clear reasoning for displaying results and avoiding any duplication of data. Where text is used, it should attempt to clarify emerging trends found in the data.

The discussion and conclusion

The discussion is arguably the most important section in any written submission of the study. Having demonstrated your knowledge of procedure and carefully outlined the method and results, it is time to interpret them. What do your results mean? What implications do they have for policy or practice, or for theoretical advancement? In this section you must present a logical and progressive argument based on the interpretation of your results in light of what we already know from previous literature. The researcher should be aware of conflicting views, evidence, and theory, and should discuss their findings in relation to this. This is also a place to discuss any limitations or deficiencies in the study. The conclusion must clearly summarise the main relevant findings in relation to the aim(s) and objectives of the study and include any recommendations for future research.

Conclusion

This chapter was designed to guide students and researchers in answering the following question: 'What options do I have for analysing the data that I have collected?' With this question in mind the chapter has unpacked the meaning of analysis and explored its various permutations. It has explained the differences that exist between quantitative and qualitative data, as well as the differences that exist within each band (e.g. quantitative research = nominal, ordinal, interval, and ratio data; qualitative research = structured text from surveys, unstructured text from interviews and observations, audio recordings, video recordings, and multimedia data).

The chapter has also explored the processes common to all forms of analysis as well as focusing attention on a variety of data analysis techniques that are commonly used in the broad discipline of sport studies. Whilst the topic coverage of this chapter does not provide an exhaustive list of analysis possibilities it does shine a light on the logic underpinning all data analysis. Methods of analysis are tools to be used by practitioners. Students and researchers simply need to know when to use them and why. Use this chapter as your guide.

References

Arijs, C., Chroni, S., Brymer, E., and Careless, D. (2017) "Leave Your Ego at the Door': A narrative investigation into effective wingsuit flying'. *Frontiers in Psychology* (8): 1–10. Available at: https://www.frontiersin.org/articles/10.3389/fpsyg.2017.01985/full

Braun, V. and Clarke, V. (2008) 'Using thematic analysis in psychology'. *Qualitative Research in Psychology*, 3 (2): 77–101.

Brown, C., Webb, T., Robinson, M. and Cotgreave, R. (2018) 'Athletes' experiences of social support during their transition out of elite sport: An Interpretive phenomenological analysis'. *Psychology of Sport and Exercise*, 36: 71–80.

Cohen, L., Manion, L. and Morrison, K. (2002) *Research Methods in Education* (5th Edition). London: Routledge.

Denzin, N. and Lincoln, Y. (2018) *Sage Handbook of Qualitative Research*. London: Sage Publications.

Dunphy, E., Hamilton, F., Spasic, I. and Button, K. (2017) 'Acceptability of a digital health intervention alongside physiotherapy to support patients following anterior cruciate ligament reconstruction'. *BMC Musculoskeletal Disorders*, 18 (1): 1–11.

Elliott, J. (2005) *Using Narratives in Social Research Methods: Qualitative and Quantitative Approaches*. London: Sage Publications.

Glaser, B. and Strauss, A. (1967) *The Discovery of Grounded Theory*. Chicago, IL: Aldane.

Gratton, C. and Jones, I. (2015) *Research Methods for Sports Studies* (3rd Edition). London: Routledge.

Gray, D. (2018) *Doing Research in the Real World* (4th Edition). London: Sage Publications.

Marshall, C. and Rossman, G. (2006) *Designing Qualitative Research* (6th Edition). London: Sage Publications.

McGannon, K., McMahon, J. and Gonsalves, C. (2016) 'Mother runners in the blogosphere: A discursive psychological analysis of online recreational athlete identities'. *Psychology of Sport and Exercise*, 28: 125–135.

Potter, J. and Wetherell, M. (1987) *Discourse and Social Psychology: Attitudes and Behaviour*. London: Sage Publications.

Rice, P. and Ezzy, D. (1999) *Qualitative Research Methods: A Health Focus*. Melbourne: Oxford University Press.

Richards, L. (2015) *Handling Qualitative Data* (3rd Edition). London: Sage Publications.

Saldana, J. (2016) *The Coding Manual for Qualitative Researchers*. London: Sage Publications.

Smith, J. and Eatough, V. (2007) 'Interpretative phenomenological analysis'. In Lyons, E. and Coyle, A. (Eds.) *Analysing Qualitative Data in Psychology*. London: Sage Publications, pp. 35–50.

Thomas, J., Nelson, J. and Silverman, S. (2015) *Research Methods in Physical Activity* (7th Edition). Champaign, IL: Human Kinetics.

Weed, M. (2009) 'Considerations for grounded theory research in sport and exercise psychology'. *Psychology of Sport and Exercise*, 10 (5): 502–510.

Westberg, K., Stavros, C., Smith, A., Munro, G. and Argus, K. (2018) 'An examination of how alcohol brands use sport to engage consumers on social media'. *Drug and Alcohol Review*, 37 (1): 28–35.

GLOSSARY

Asynchronous interviews   refers to interviews that are not conducted live.

Blog   a regularly updated website typically administered by one person or a small group of people.

Closed survey questions   limit the options available for participants to respond to a question.

Coding   as researchers analyse the data, a coding process takes place. Codes are the labels which refer to the fresh ideas and themes that begin to emerge out of the data.

Complete participant observation   researchers adopting this position hide their true identity and motives from the group. By doing so, it is hoped that their presence is taken for granted and the group's behaviour returns to 'normal'.

Confidentiality   information collected that is to be kept private and secret and not for public disclosure.

Content analysis   the analysis of information gathered from platforms such as online newspaper databases, online fan forums, social media sites, and so on. The data is usually coded and themes are created.

Convenience sampling   potential participants are selected because access to them is conveniently available.

Cross-tabulations   a method of analysis used to analyse the relationship between multiple variables to understand the correlations between different variables.

Data cleaning   detecting and then correcting or removing incomplete, incorrect, irrelevant, or inaccurate aspects of the data.

Data saturation   the point in the data collection process where the analysis of the data already collected indicates no new information will change the findings of the study.

Deductive reasoning   conducting research in order to test the hypothesis or theory.

Descriptive statistics describes the basic features of the results by providing a statistical summary of individual questions on the survey.

Dissertation an extended essay which many undergraduate and postgraduate students write.

Elicited research relies on direct interaction with informants as researchers elicit participant's responses to questions or other prompts.

Emoticons a term that is short for emotion icon. It is a pictorial representation of a facial expression using characters – usually punctuation marks, numbers, and letters to denote a person's feelings or mood.

Empirical research generates and tests out new ideas through the collection and critical examination of primary data.

Enacted research refers to an activity or event which is constructed by the researcher that allows the data to flow, such as role-plays, simulations, or games.

Epistemology a branch of philosophy that investigates the origin, nature, methods, and limits of human knowledge.

Essentialist method emphasises the experiences, meanings, and the reality for participants.

Ethics moral principles, values, and obligations that govern or regulate a person's behaviour or conduct.

Ethnography the observation of groups or cultures whereby the researcher becomes immersed within the field. Additional methods often feature in order to test the researcher's observations.

Extant research the reading, copying, or downloading of data that is already available online.

Field the broad area in which the researcher intends to study, such as social media, football fandom, or the Olympics.

FtF face to face.

Gatekeepers the sponsors, or advocates, of your research project. These figures are often influential and are able to introduce you to the group or people under investigation.

Harm the causing of physical, psychological, or social distress through an action.

Hermeneutics a theory and methodology of interpretation.

Idiographic pertaining to or involving the study of individual cases or events.

Immersion long-term observation, thus categorised as ethnography or netnography, relies on immersion. This is where the researcher spends several hours a day within the research community under investigation for a prolonged period of time.

Inductive reasoning researchers analyse data free from preconceived ideas, hypothesis, or theories. Observations are used to create theory rather than test it.

Inferential statistics researchers try to reach conclusions that extend beyond the immediate data. Thus, inferential statistics are used to make inferences from data to more general populations.

Informed consent   the providing of permission by a participant in full knowledge of what their participation in the research project will involve and any associated risks that may occur.

Insider   refers to researchers who become immersed within the communities being investigated. They gather research from the 'inside'. Insiders are otherwise called emic researchers.

Interval data   specifies that the distances between each value on the scale are equal.

IP address   a unique identifier written as a numerical label that is assigned to any device connected to the internet that communicates with other devices.

Memos   informal records that are held by the research team to help them shape their ideas.

Multi-modal   refers to the many variations of communication practices in contemporary societies.

Multiple regression   when researchers want to predict the value of a variable based on the value of two or more other variables.

Netiquette   refers to rules of etiquette that apply when communicating online.

Netnography   an ethnographic tool employed when investigating social interaction in online spaces.

Nominal data   data items which are differentiated by a simple naming system. Whilst numbers may be assigned to the data they are simply used to categorise. Beyond this there is no meaningful quantitative value.

Nomothetic   relating to the discovery of general scientific laws.

Non-parametric tests   statistical tests used when the data being analysed is not normally distributed.

Non-participant observation   otherwise called direct observation, this is an unobtrusive approach to observation. The researcher usually designs a structured approach to observation whereby a quantifiable coding schedule is in place.

Normal distribution   a statistical test that calculates how closely all data points are gathered around the mean value in the data set. It is characterised by a bell-shaped curve symmetrical around the mean value.

Objective research   research that is considered pure, meaning that the researcher themselves, or external parties, have had little to no influence over the research process or the generated data.

Observation   the observation of groups, people, or spaces when investigating a specific phenomenon. Observation can take place online or offline and this term is preferred to describe research in which the data collection stage has been short-term, rather than long-term.

Open survey questions   allow the participant to respond without word restriction to a question. They are also not limited by a prescribed set of options.

Ordinal data   for data to be classified as ordinal the data must feature an orderly scale but the difference between each data point is not known.

Originality all new research must attempt to offer something different to what has previously been published. Original research may build on prior work, draw comparisons with them, challenge existing work, and so on.

Outsider a research position central to observation and ethnography whereby the researcher remains a detached, impartial onlooker throughout the investigation. Outsiders are otherwise called etic researchers.

Parametric tests statistical tests that can be used when a data set is normally distributed.

Participant information sheet a document provided to participants detailing an overview of the research project, their role as a participant, the ethical process, and the researcher's contact details, thus allowing them to make an informed choice about whether to participate or not.

Participant observation the researcher announces themselves to their informants from the beginning, usually with the aid of gatekeepers who grant and facilitate their entry into the respective community. Researchers employing this approach therefore gather data from the inside, rather than the outside.

Phenomenology a philosophic method of inquiry involving the systematic investigation of consciousness.

Phenomenon an occurrence that is observed to happen.

Population relates to the entire possible sample which could feature in a study.

Primary source refers to data that has been gathered for a specific project.

Pseudonym the use of a fictitious name to protect the identity of the participant.

Qualitative the emphasis is on 'quality' data. This methodological approach aims to understand the how and the why. It gathers rich data and tends to use smaller samples.

Quantitative the emphasis is on producing quantifiable results, so researchers can highlight what is happening, rather than why it is happening. These methods are often used to make generalisations.

Rapport striving for a harmonious relationship where the researcher understands the feelings and needs of the research participant and can communicate effectively.

Ratio data interval data with a natural zero point.

Reflexive thinking with a purpose, being critical, reflecting on the issue under study, questioning, probing, and making judgements in a considered and measured way.

Reflexivity relates to researchers being critical of their identities during the research process and how their self may affect their interpretations of the data.

Research aim refers to the researcher's overall research goals. The aim(s) relate to what they want to achieve, not how they will achieve it.

Research objectives refers to what researchers want to accomplish in the project. The list of objectives should be highly focused and closely related to the research aim(s).

Respondent validation otherwise known as a member check is a technique used by researchers to help improve the accuracy, credibility, and, transferability of a study. It involves feeding back findings to participants to see if they have been interpreted accurately.

Rigour   strong when the research team have applied the appropriate research tools to meet the stated objectives of the project.

Sampling   a sample refers to a group of people, objects or spaces that are identified from a larger population. There are two main types of sampling approaches: probability and non-probability. The former includes random and stratified approaches, while the latter includes convenience and critical sampling.

Saturation   the point in the research whereby no new information or themes are being generated.

Secondary source   a source which has already been published. Research projects that decide to just use secondary sources are often called 'literature based' projects.

Self-selection sampling   where individuals select themselves to be part of a study rather than being identified by the researcher.

Semi-structured   often associated with interviews that are only partially organised or structured.

Skip pattern   often used in online surveys, where the participant is directed to a different set of questions based on an earlier answer given in the survey (such as male or female; smoker or non-smoker; player, fan, coach, referee).

Social constructionist   a perspective that many of the characteristics and groups that shape society are inventions of the people living within it. Researchers who adopt this position form a critical stance towards the taken for granted ways that we understand the world and ourselves.

SPSS   a software package used for statistical analysis.

Standard deviation   a measure that is used to quantify the variation of a set of data values.

Steering group   made up of experts who oversee a research project to ensure that protocols are followed and provide advice and troubleshoot when called upon.

Synchronous interviews   existing or occurring at the same time. Synchronous interviews take place live, in real time.

Theoretical research   relies on the critical examination of findings from secondary sources and using it to develop or shape new theories and explanations.

Topic   a research topic gives a study an angle or focus. This is often generated once the literature has been consulted.

Triangulation   the use of more than one method to double or cross check the research findings.

Unstructured   refers to interviews without any formal organisation or structure.

Validity   a process to assess the rigour of the research. When assessing validity, we ask, 'does the research achieve what it set out to?' 'Does it measure what it set out to measure?'

VoIP a category of hardware and software that enables people to use the internet as the transmission medium for telephone calls by sending voice data along with live images.

Wiki a knowledge base website on which users collaboratively modify the content and structure directly from the web browser.

Working title a flexible research question that may change during the research project.

INDEX

abstract 136
access 12
analysis 113
asynchronous online interviews 75–80;
    advantages 79–80; limitations 80;
    practical advice 76–77; procedure 76
attrition rates 80

blogs 75

coding 32, 34, 105, 114
content analysis 124–127

data saturation 59
discourse analysis 127–128
discussion and conclusion 137
dissertation 11

emoticons 77
ethics 54, 59, 67, 101–102; 107, 109–110;
    deception 47; ethical process 40–42;
    good practice 51; harm 44, 46–47;
    informed consent 42–46, 48, 54 (children
    43); participation information sheet 44,
    54, 59; pseudonyms 44, 46; public *vs.*
    private data 43, 48–49, 57, 67; right of
    withdrawal 43, 44
ethnography: defining 30, 93; origins
    93–94; types (audience 96; auto-
    ethnographic 96; critical realist 96;
    institutional 96; performative 97; sensory
    97; visual 97)

gatekeepers 32, 102
grounded theory 15, 134–135

interpretive phenomenological analysis
    128–130
interviews 72–75; email 75; semi-structured
    74; structured interviews 73–74;
    unstructured 74–75
introduction 136

literature review 21–23, 33, 136

methodological approach 136

narrative analysis 130–132
netnography: advantages 106; advice
    108–109; defining 97–98; disadvantages
    106–107; elicited 98; enacted 98; entrée
    41, 43, 48, 57, 101–103; extant 98; field
    notes 104, 109; immersion 47, 99–101,
    107; scratch notes 104

objectivity 28, 105, 107
observation types: complete 95; direct 94;
    participant 94–95; reflexivity 104
online interviews (preparation) 85–90;
    interview guide 87; netiquette 86–87;
    preparing probes 88–89 (attention
    probes 88; change of direction probes
    88; clarification probes 88; conversation
    management probes 88; non-verbal
    probes 89; practice 89–90; retrospective

elaboration probes 88); recruiting participants 85; representative samples 85–86

online sources 23–26; blogs 24; e-books 23; email 25; journals 23; newspaper 24; search engines 24; social media 24; statistics 24; streaming platforms 24; validity 25–26; vlogs 24; Wikipedia 25

online surveys 43, 44; advantages 68; analysis 64; conducting an online survey 65–66; coverage error and non-response 67–68; data cleaning 68; data saturation 59; disadvantages 69; email 55, 65, 67; IP address 68; participant recruitment 65; pilot study 65, 66; planning and developing 55; questions (open and closed) 59–62, 64–65 (skip pattern 62); sampling 56–57, 59; web-based 55, 65, 66, 67

originality 9, 14, 16

phenomenon 72, 73

qualitative research: characteristics 27–28; general stages 120 (coding (first stage) 121; coding (second stage) 123; immersion 120; interpreting codes 124; memos 122; saturation 22, 123; transcription 120); insider 102; outsider 102; qualitative data analysis 105, 119

quantitative research 114–119; characteristics 27–28; chi square 118; Cramer coefficient 117; factor analysis 118; interval data 117; Kendall rank correlation coefficient 116; Komogarov-Smirnov 116; Kruskal-Wallis test 117; logical regression 118; Mann-Whitney U test 116; multiple regression 118; nominal data 115; non-parametric tests 116–117; one group T-test 118; one-way analysis of variance 118; ordinal data 115; Pearson's correlation coefficient 118; Spearman's Rho 118; SPSS 117

rapport 77

reflexivity 96, 109

research: aims 17; field 8, 10, 14, 17; objectives 17; positionality 94–95, 103, 108; question 17, 22; timeline 17, 33–35; topic 8, 10, 14, 17

research types: comparative 18, 24; convert 101; Critical Race Theory (CRT) 20; descriptive 18–19; empirical 21; explanatory 19; exploratory 18; feminist 20; historical 18, 24; impact 13–14, 19–20; opportunistic 101; predictive 19; primary 21; secondary 21; theoretical 21

results 137

rigour 124

sampling 56–57, 59; types 31–33 (cluster 31; convenience 32, 56, 57; critical 32; emergent 32; nominated 32; non-probability 31–32, 56, 59; opportunistic 32; population 31–32; probability 31, 56, 57; random 31; self-selection 56; snowball 32, 56; stratified 31; systematic 31; theoretical 32; typical 33)

saturation 123

standard deviation 117

subjectivity 105, 107

synchronous online interviews 81, 98; challenges 84–85; text-based 81–82; video interviews 82–85; VoIP technologies 82

thematic analysis 41, 132–134

time management 11–12, 35

triangulation 124

validity 114

wikis 75

working title 14, 17

For Product Safety Concerns and Information please contact our EU
representative GPSR@taylorandfrancis.com
Taylor & Francis Verlag GmbH, Kaufingerstraße 24, 80331 München, Germany